'There are no stupid questions, nor any forbidden ones, but there are some questions that have no answer.'

Hédi Fried was nineteen when the Nazis snatched her family from their home in Eastern Europe and transported them to Auschwitz, where her parents were murdered and she and her sister were forced into hard labour until the end of the war.

Now ninety-four, she has spent her life educating young people about the Holocaust and answering their questions about one of the darkest periods in human history. Questions like, 'How was it to live in the camps?', 'Why did Hitler hate the Jews?', and 'Can you forgive?'.

With sensitivity and complete candour, Fried answers these questions and more in this deeply human book that urges us never to forget and never to repeat.

Questions I am asked about the Holocaust

For all the young people around the world

Questions
I am asked
about the
Holocaust

Hédi Fried

Translated from the Swedish
by Alice E. Olsson

SCRIBE
Melbourne • London

Scribe Publications
2 John St, Clerkenwell, London, WC1N 2ES, United Kingdom
18–20 Edward St, Brunswick, Victoria 3056, Australia
3754 Pleasant Ave, Suite 100, Minneapolis, Minnesota 55409 USA

Originally published in Swedish as *Frågor jag fått om Förintelsen*
by Natur & Kultur in 2017
Published by agreement with Partners in Stories Stockholm AB
First published in English by Scribe in 2019

Typeset in Garamond Premier by the publishers.

Printed and bound in the UK by CPI Group (UK) Ltd, Croydon CR0 4YY

Scribe Publications is committed to the sustainable use of natural resources
and the use of paper products made responsibly from those resources.

9781911617778 (UK edition)
9781925713800 (Australian edition)
9781947534599 (US edition)
9781925693447 (e-book)

The cost of this translation was de
Arts Council, gratefully acknowle

CiP records for this title are availa
National Library of Australia.

scribepublications.co.uk
scribepublications.com.au
scribepublications.com

När sorgen kommer, som när natten skymmer
i vilda skogen, där en man går vill,
vem tror på ljuset, som i fjärran rymmer,
Och sken som skymta fram och flämta till?
På skämt de glimta och på skämt de flykta,
vem tar en lyktman för en man med lykta?

When sorrow comes, as when night falls
in the wild woods, where a man goes astray,
who believes in the light that in the distance calls,
And the glow that appears and then fades away?
In jest does it fade and in jest does it burn,
who takes a lantern-man for a man with a lantern?

'Solace', Gustaf Fröding,
translated by Alice E. Olsson

Contents

Preface

Many years have passed since I wrote my autobiography, *Fragments of a Life: the road to Auschwitz,* and the subsequent books. Since then, I have lectured in schools and universities with the strong conviction that the younger generation must keep the memory of the Holocaust alive if we want to ensure that it is never repeated. What has happened once may unfortunately happen again, if not in exactly the same way. To prevent this, it is important to remember; the past leaves its mark on the present and casts its shadow over the future.

In the beginning of September 1940, Northern Transylvania was returned to Hungary from Romania. At first, I was in despair. The persecution of Jews began, although there was not yet a direct threat to our lives. It did not take long, however, until news came from Romania that Jews there were being sent to Ukraine, where they were forced to dig their own graves before being shot. Then I was happy that we belonged to Hungary. I grew accustomed to our reduced circumstances, and was glad that we were no longer under Romanian rule. I can still see myself knitting woollen socks for the poor souls who were transported in freezing trains from Romania to Ukraine, in the middle of winter, who had not been allowed to bring any warm clothing. Then came March 1944, the invasion of the Germans, and now I had every reason to mourn that we no longer belonged to Romania. The Romanians did not hand over their Jews to the Germans; instead they were paid $100 for every person who was allowed to leave for Israel.

In the end, I was one of the lucky ones. I was lucky many times over.

My luck began at the time of our arrival to Auschwitz, where my sister and I survived the selection and were spared from the gas chambers. Fortuitous events then repeated themselves several times during my year in captivity. Most importantly, I did not end up in one of the worst labour camps.

From Auschwitz, I was sent to three different labour camps, where we were usually tasked with clearing up among the ruins. Many others were placed in camps where they had to work in shifts in underground factories, mines, or quarries. Several times, I found myself in situations when I was certain that my last moment had come, but something happened, and I survived.

In the camps, you never knew if a change would mean life or death. Though sometimes you don't know that in everyday life, either. We live a quiet life, the days go by, we don't notice anything. The change occurs little by little until the picture is suddenly clear and we wonder: how could this have happened? Life teaches us that everything can change in a moment, and you never know beforehand whether the change is going to lead to something better or worse.

My school lectures usually consist of three parts, with emphasis on the third. They start with an attempt to portray the people of the past and their living conditions, which contributed to making the Holocaust possible; they continue with the story of my own experiences; and they end with ample time for questions.

I stress that there are no stupid questions, nor any forbidden ones, but that some questions have no answer. There is, for example, no single answer to the question 'Why did the Holocaust happen?' This makes the other questions surrounding it all the more important.

I have gathered the most common questions that I am asked in this book, to help those who want to know more about the Holocaust. My hope is that it will be read by and benefit the young people of today and of tomorrow.

The aim of this book is to teach us to avoid historical mistakes. I hope that it can make everyone who reads it see that we are not predestined to step into the role of either perpetrator or bystander. As individuals, we have a will and a responsibility, and only by taking that responsibility can we avoid history repeating itself once again.

Hédi Fried, December 2016 (updated July 2018)

'What is the worst thing that has happened to you?'

If you are asking what the single worst thing that has happened to me is, I can answer with one sentence: the moment I was separated from my parents.

But I want to give a longer answer; I will tell you about the road that led there. The Germans' planned extermination of the Jews was a very slow process, very cleverly calculated. Just as the eye cannot observe the gradual metamorphosis of a flower from bud to rose in full bloom, we too did not notice the small, almost imperceptible steps that would lead, eventually, to the full execution of their plan — to that which you could not imagine, even in your wildest dreams. All of a sudden, a change for the worse was introduced, but you could live with it. It would pass, we thought. It did not pass. Instead, there was another change. Once again, we reacted by hoping that it too would soon pass. We never knew what the next change would be or when it would come.

Despite everything I have been through, I was lucky. The worst thing that could happen to a person did not happen to me. To begin with, I was not caught in the Germans' net until the eleventh hour of the war, the spring of 1944, when the majority of Europe's Jews had already been taken prisoner.

I was born in Sighet, a small town in Romania, in the northern part of Transylvania, an area that Hungarians and Romanians have been fighting over for many centuries. Even today, both consider themselves to have a claim on the region. Before the First World War, the area was Hungarian and belonged to the Austro-Hungarian monarchy. After the Treaty of Trianon in 1920, it passed to Romania, and when the Second World War broke out there was pressure from Germany to return the area to Hungary. In September 1940, the Hungarians marched into Northern Transylvania and our fate was sealed.

Some of the Nuremberg Laws were implemented immediately, which meant that the financial situation for the Jews became increasingly dire. Jewish public servants were dismissed. Jewish doctors and lawyers were only allowed to treat and represent other Jews. Non-Jews were not allowed to shop at Jewish stores. Schools and universities were closed to Jewish children. It was bad, but our lives were not threatened. And you can get used to anything.

One of the lessons from the Holocaust is this: never get used to injustice. An injustice is like a grain of sand in your hand; on its own, its weight may seem insignificant, but injustices have a tendency to multiply, they soon become so heavy that you can no longer bear them. And it would still be some time before the next injustice came to pass.

We cut our coats according to our cloth, and considering what was happening in Germany and the rest of the world, we were happy that we still lived without imminent danger to our lives.

Hitler found it difficult to accept that Hungary's 800,000 Jews were still living in reasonable comfort, and demanded their extradition. In the beginning, the Hungarian head of state Miklós Horthy refused, but he was arrested, and the Germans appointed the leader of the Nazi Arrow Cross movement, Ferenc Szálasi, as prime minister. Szálasi also wanted to get rid of the Jews, and on 19 March 1944 the border was opened to the German troops.

From that day on, things began to happen very quickly. Immediately, Hungarian Jews were ordered to fashion a yellow star and wear it stitched to their clothes when in public. Jews were not allowed in the streets, other than when running urgent errands; they were not to stop and speak to each other, not to go to the cinema, not to eat in restaurants, not to linger in parks. These things simply had to be accepted; disobedience would be punished by death. It was, once again, just another step, and everyone hoped that there would not be more. But there were.

Barely four weeks later, we were informed that, as early as the following day, the relocation of the town's Jews would begin. All the Jews would be moved, street by street, to the newly designated ghetto in the northern part of town. Our street was the first. You were allowed to bring what you could carry; wheelbarrows were permitted.

As we began to pack, I walked around and said farewell to the things I found it hard to leave behind. First, I hid my diaries under the ridge of the roof, then I played one last time on the piano, and caressed the lid as I closed it. I ran my eyes over the bookcase, stroked my printed companions, and went out into the yard to hug Bodri, our loyal guard dog. I tried to calm both him and myself with the thought that the neighbour surely would not forget to take care of him. Back in the house, I stopped in front of the photographs of my grandparents and asked them to guard our home while we were away.

I was convinced that it was only a matter of time before we would be back. The war was no longer going very well for the Germans; Russia had turned out to be a tougher nut to crack than they had thought. In my naïvety, I thought that soon the Germans would lose, Romania would regain possession of its territories, everything would be back to normal, and I could return to university.

The next morning, I awoke to reality. The *gendarmes* (village police) came, Papa locked up, put the key in his pocket, and we were taken to the ghetto. Now, an even more difficult time began. But once again, you had to get used to it. And the hope for a swift end to the war was still there.

Again, barely four weeks had passed — only two months since the invasion of the Germans — before we heard the drummer on the corner of the street beat his drum and call out: 'Attention, attention! The Jews are to be moved from the ghetto. They shall pack 20 kilos each and stand in front of their gate tomorrow, ready for *Abtransport*, to be taken away.'

Where? No one knew. Mama was in despair. 'They will kill us,' she said, weeping.

I could not accept her defeatism and replied, 'No, why would they, we haven't done anything. You'll see that we'll be sent to inner Hungary to work in the fields. The men are all at the front, they need the labour for the spring sowing.'

And Mama allowed herself to be comforted.

What do you bring when you are only allowed 20 kilograms? Mama packed mostly food, things that would keep. We put on several layers of clothing, and sturdy shoes. I myself packed a small bag with a set of underwear, my diary, and a book of poems by my favourite poet, Attila József. We could not anticipate that even this, our last possession, would be taken from us.

The next morning, we stood outside the gate with our luggage. We were made to stand in rows of five and were marched off through the streets of the town towards the train station, where the cattle cars were waiting.

'For eight horses' it said on the side of the car, and we were hustled inside, a hundred in each. It was packed and it was dark. Only one little hole let through some light and air. We huddled up as best we could, but still there was not enough room for everyone to sit. Two buckets to relieve ourselves in and two buckets of water were placed inside, the sliding doors were pulled shut and locked, and the train started running. The journey took three days and three nights under the most abhorrent of circumstances. It was punctuated by intermittent stops, while the stench and thirst became unbearable. We begged for help to no avail. But nothing happened until the night of 17 May. That was when we arrived at Auschwitz.

'Why did Hitler hate the Jews?'

I remember a macabre joke that was told during the war. Jacob asks Daniel: 'Who started the war?' and Daniel answers: 'The Jews and the cyclists.' 'Why the cyclists?' asks Jacob. 'Why the Jews?' Daniel replies.

Growing up, I slowly became aware of the world outside my little room, the big world. That other children lived in different conditions, that not everyone spoke the same language, that not everyone went to the synagogue like I did. As I grew older, I understood more of my parents' conversations, and I began to feel afraid. What was happening? My parents talked about politics, about the coming elections and the risk that us Jews would be in trouble if the anti-Semitic farmers' party won. The liberals were still in power, and I was mighty proud that Papa's oldest brother was a member of parliament. At the same time, I listened in on discussions about Germany, the country far away, where a party that persecuted Jews was in power. 'Why?' I asked.

My father told me about the history of anti-Semitism. How, far back in time, people believed in many different gods. In Ur, in Mesopotamia, there was a small tribe led by a man named Terah, an idol maker. His son Abraham doubted that some lifeless lumps of clay could rule the world. He arrived at the conviction that there must be an invisible higher power. A new religion was born — monotheism, the belief in one true God — and Abraham became its founding father. The religion was given the name Judaism, and it spread. But the rest of the world had a hard time accepting it.

After the birth of Christ, a new kind of monotheism began to spread. It was known as Christianity. Jesus himself was a Jew, a rabbi in one of the various Jewish factions. Soon, more people followed Jesus' doctrine, and his disciples went out into the world to convert heathens. The Christian prophets tried to convince the Jews to adopt Christianity, but when the Jews steadfastly refused, they were accused of having murdered Christ. The persecution of the Jews took increasingly hateful forms.

Various unfounded accusations began to spread and witch-hunts of Jews became commonplace over the centuries. Two of these accusations in particular have survived until today, despite the fact that their groundlessness has been proven time and time again.

One of them is that Jews murder little children and use their blood to bake bread for Easter. The first time this rumour spread was in the Middle Ages, in a village in Eastern Europe. One day in early spring, a young Christian boy disappeared, and the Jewish baker in the village was accused of having slaughtered the child to use his blood for the Easter bread. False witnesses were lined up, who claimed to have seen the incident. That was enough for the villagers to initiate a pogrom: they armed themselves with cudgels and marched on the Jews, ready to murder every last one of them.

Later, when the ice on the top of the nearby lake melted, the child's dead body floated to the surface. But that did not help. Soon, the next village would make the same accusation when a child went through the ice. The last trial on the basis of such an allegation was held in 1883 in Hungary.

The other unfounded accusation was a concoction of lies originating in Tsarist Russia, compiled in a pamphlet titled *The Protocols of the Elders of Zion*. This was a fabrication about how the Jews held various leading positions all over the world. In a meeting at the end of the nineteenth century, it claimed, they had drawn up a detailed plan for achieving global domination. Hitler took this paranoid old wives' tale as blood-tainted truth; it led to his fear of the Jews, and expressed itself through aggressive hatred and his determination to exterminate every last one of them.

Hitler's hatred for the Jews was so strong that you could say that he was not waging war against the Allies, but against the Jews. Even when there were no more train seats left for transporting soldiers to the front, he continued to mobilise carriages for the transport of Jews to Auschwitz.

Paradoxically, the German population at large was not anti-Semitic. There was therefore a strong need to foster anti-Semitism among the people, and Goebbels, the minister of propaganda, was ingenious at this. Film, art, literature, education — everything was permeated by anti-Semitic doctrine. Prejudices were cemented, and every German child was taught that the Jews were not people, they were to be destroyed. Jews were vermin to be exterminated, Jews were a cancerous growth on the clean body of the Reich, and the cancer had to be excised.

A simple answer to the question: Hitler hated the Jews because they were Jews.

'What was your life like before the war?'

Life in the quiet little town of Sighet was fairly uneventful. The town's 30,000 or so inhabitants were made up of countless ethnic minorities, of which the Jews were the most numerous. When I think about it, a few events surface in my memory that illustrate what life was like:

I was three years old and had started preschool. I felt grown up, and after a few days I insisted that no one was to collect me; I wanted to walk home on my own. Mama did not want to agree to it, but in the end my stubbornness triumphed. It was midday and the cluster of little children stood by the gate, on their way home, with me in the middle. Some were going right, some left. I was eagerly absorbed in a discussion with an older friend and did not think about which way I should take to get home. Without looking around, I followed my friend and joined the cluster turning left.

As we walked, I noticed that more and more of the children veered off, until only my friend and I were left, chatting away. But soon the words froze on my lips, when she too stopped by a gate. I was completely alone. Only then did I look around and see that I did not know where I was. I became scared, realising that I was lost. I started crying.

A woman leaned out of a window and asked why I was crying. I answered that I did not know my way home.

'What's your name?' she asked.

'Hédike,' I replied.

'Whose are you?'

'Papa's.'

'Where do you live?'

'In a house with a red gate.'

'Don't cry, Hédike,' the woman continued, 'I'll take you home.' The town was small enough that she could recognise me, as I resembled my father.

Most people in Sighet knew each other even if they did not socialise. Life went by in similar ways among the different social groups, which were determined by class, rather than ethnicity. There were the very poor and the slightly wealthier. Our family belonged to the latter. Everyone in that group had domestic help; today you might call it a maid.

Anna, our maid, got up as early as six o'clock. She lit a fire in the stove so that we would not have to rise in a freezing room. Anna had to coax us up; we were cold and did not want to get out of bed. Then she dressed us, fed us breakfast, and took us to school. Only then did my parents get up. After breakfast, Papa went to work and Mama went to the market to do the shopping.

'When did you realise that your family was in danger?'

I cannot remember when I became aware that my family could be in danger. But when I did, I knew it was the kind of danger that all Jews faced, not just our family. The thought must have been taking root for a long time before it reached the surface of my consciousness in my teens.

It started when I was 14 years old and in love with a man who worked at the post office. Rumours of war were in the air, and schools were training young people to be of use in case conflict broke out. We were allowed to choose a field in which we would learn to be helpful. Some chose the hospital to learn nursing, others the police force, and I wanted to go into the postal service.

We were six students who walked over to the post office, led by our art teacher. I was happy and excited.

I was on my way to see my sweetheart and would be learning Morse code, something I was very keen on. We were greeted by the postmaster, who welcomed us ceremoniously, explaining the uncertain political climate and the importance of the postal service in this context. How everything that happens at the post office is classified ... Here, he broke off sharply, looked around, and said, 'I presume that everyone in this room is Romanian?'

The teacher looked at me and said, hesitantly, 'Nooo, not everyone.'

The postmaster put down the paper in his hand and said, 'In that case, we can't continue.' We had to go home.

I came home that day howling, and Mama was terrified. She feared the worst. 'What's happened?' she asked, over and over again. I just kept sobbing. Finally, I managed to tell her. I was so angry and humiliated that I wanted Mama to promise me that we would leave the country. I could not keep living in a place that looked down on me, that saw me as a second-class citizen. Meanwhile, Papa also came home for lunch, and both of them had their hands full trying to comfort me, to make me change my mind. They tried to explain that we did not have anywhere to go, that anti-Semitism exists in all the countries of the world, and as long as we did not have a country of our own, we had no choice; we had to get used to it. I did not want to get used to it, I was not going to accept it, but eventually I calmed down. That was probably my first awakening.

As time passed, the threat came ever closer. The Jews were in danger, and that included my family. I cannot remember any conscious fear. It was, rather, an inexplicable, dull yet unremitting pressure in my chest, sometimes more intense, sometimes weaker, but it never let up. A human being does not want to believe that wicked things may happen to her. I, too, wanted to believe the officer from the SS (Hitler's elite police force) who told my father that everything he'd heard about the persecution of Jews was just rumours; Germans are civilised people, he said.

Sometimes, I think about what Mama said about getting used to it, and how easy it is.

I will never get used to it, I said then. But when I look back, that is exactly what I did. A human being's will to live is so strong that she will not give up until she can feel the knife's edge against her throat. And by then she may have become so apathetic that she simply thinks to herself: 'It doesn't matter, just let it be quick.' That was what I thought when, as we arrived at

Auschwitz, I was told by a male prisoner that we had entered an extermination camp. So it was death that lay in store? Let it be quick, then.

Later, when I was separated from my mother, a feeling of relief crept into me. I realised that the young were being spared. But at the same time, a heavy sorrow washed over me. 'Mama, what is going to happen to my mama?' And to this day, I still dare not carry that thought to its conclusion.

Injustices must be nipped in the bud. In Germany, there should have been protests by the beginning of the 1930s. Only a couple of years later, it was too late.

'How could an entire people get behind Hitler?'

The racism that led to the Holocaust has roots stretching far back in time. It is about keeping the flock together, about greed and fear. These were the emotions that Hitler exploited to recruit members to the Nazi Party.

Hitler's rousing speeches called for unity within the great German race, the reconquering of lost lands, and fear of a Jewish world conspiracy that encompassed both capitalism and communism. People were unhappy with the situation in Germany at the time, with weak politicians and high unemployment. Hitler played upon the feeling of betrayal that many Germans felt at the end of the First World War: the humiliated Fatherland and the people's suffering that demanded restitution. He called for national unity, promising bread and work.

In the beginning of the 1930s, Nazism did not have very many followers. Thanks to the charisma and power of speech that Hitler possessed, however, more and more people began to join him. These were people from all layers of society — industrialists and business leaders who thought they could profit from his politics, military men who liked his racist ideas, ordinary people who were tired of poverty, and women who fell for his charm.

Hitler exerted a hypnotic force on the women, and they became his most loyal voters. It seems strange today, as according to him the women's role could be summarised as 'K. K. K.', that is, *Kinder, Küche, Kirche*. Children, Kitchen, Church.

Hitler had skilful people to help him. They targeted young people, and devised powerful propaganda through film, literature, and art. Jews were caricatured, placed on a level with pests and vermin. The anti-Semitic propaganda was aimed at all age groups: it started by targeting little children, continued in school textbooks, and ended with literature and films for adults. To this day, Leni Riefenstahl's *Triumph of the Will* is seen as a prototype for effective propaganda.

In textbooks, there were elements of propaganda in every subject. The following maths problem from a high school textbook published in 1935 is just one example: 'How many government loans would it be possible to give to newly-weds for the amount of money the government spends on taking care of the disabled, the criminals, and the insane?'

Great emphasis was placed on the physical education of young people; they were to be hardened both physically and mentally. They were recruited into *Hitlerjugend* (the Hitler Youth), where camp life and camaraderie turned them into the Führer's most loyal lackeys. The girls had their own sub-group, *Bund Deutscher Mädel* (the League of German Girls), where they were trained to be model citizens, and raised to become mothers of many children.

Despite growing support for Hitler, the population at large was not anti-Semitic. Few were seduced by the anti-Semitic propaganda. Some joined the party because they wanted to try something new, others because of peer pressure.

One man, a young law student at the time, explained to me how two of his good friends and colleagues, who had both initially been completely against Hitler, slowly turned. One of them justified it by saying that none of the other parties had a solution to the poor political and financial situation, and that it might therefore be time to try something new. The other was drawn in by the ever-increasing number of party members, and began to think 'the masses can't be wrong'. The then-student who told me the story never let himself be influenced; he moved abroad instead. With time, fewer and fewer objected.

'Why did you not fight back?'

Actively fighting back in 1944 would have been suicide. There should have been active resistance *before* the Nazis gained power. But passive resistance could still be found in Sighet. Communist cells were organised on the sly. It was all very secretive, and I, the youngest member, was allowed to participate in the ideological training. I read Marx and Engels, and soon I was a dedicated communist who, rather than reciting the evening prayer that Grandfather had taught me, now hummed 'The Internationale' at bedtime. In communism, we saw our only potential salvation from Nazism, and many young people fled across the border to the neighbouring Soviet Union, partly in the hope of being rescued, but also partly in the hope of being able to actively fight the Germans from behind Soviet lines.

One day in the late 1940s, after the war had ended,

the doorbell rang at my house in Aspudden, Sweden. I answered it, and was met by two young men I did not recognise. They introduced themselves as Moishi Kaufmann and David Stern, former workers in my father's small cardboard factory. I remembered one of them — he was among those who had fled to the Soviet Union. I had always envied him for daring to leave and thereby escaping the Holocaust. Now, I got to hear an entirely different story.

One night, he and his friend had hiked up into Solovan, a foothill of the Carpathian Mountains, to meet up with a guide who was going help them cross the border into the Soviet Union. After paying him with the last of their savings, they groped their way through the dense, dark forest. They hid during the day and slept for a few hours, continuing at night. After three days, they reached the border, where the guide gave them instructions for their onwards journey. From there, they had to find their own way, simply continuing until they reached the valley below, where freedom awaited. They kept going, but the forest seemed as if it would never end. They lost their way, ran out of provisions, and had not yet seen a living soul. After a couple of days, they were stopped by border guards who asked questions, and took them straight to prison.

Their explanation — that they were Jews, dedicated communists fleeing from the Germans — did nothing. The Russians thought that they were German spies. Without further explanation, they were put on a train with several hundred others, and after a many-weeks-long journey, they were deposited in Vorkuta, in deepest Siberia.

Much later, after having suffered through several years of the most difficult conditions imaginable, they finally managed to flee the camp. Eventually, they reached Finland, where they found out that the war was already over. They made their way to Sweden, and now they were in Stockholm, waiting to travel to Palestine.

While some left for the Soviet Union, another way of putting up passive resistance was to hide in the mountains. There were a few people in Sighet who tried, but none of them succeeded. They were sold out by anti-Semitic farmers who saw a possibility to make some money.

By the time we reached the camp, most of us were too apathetic to put up a fight. No one had the strength to think, you simply followed orders. You clung to life, no matter how difficult it seemed. It was not until the prisoners perceived the situation to be utterly hopeless, ending in death either way, that they actively fought back.

The prisoners in Sobibór attempted to break out of the camp. They were only partly successful. Some managed to escape, but most of them were shot or died some other way in the surrounding woods.

In Warsaw, it became clear that the entire ghetto would be liquidated, and that no one would escape transportation to the gas chambers. With the help of weapons smuggled into the ghetto by the Polish resistance movement, the prisoners held their ground for 40 days. A few managed to escape through the sewers. In the end, the SS set fire to the ghetto, and only 20 survivors were led out.

In the autumn of 1944, the *Sonderkommando* — the prisoners who worked in crematoriums 3 and 4 in Auschwitz — decided to blow up the buildings. They knew that they would be gassed regardless: the men in the *Sonderkommando* were routinely replaced every six months; they knew too much to be allowed to live. They made contact with six girls who worked in the neighbouring ammunitions factory, and asked them to smuggle in some explosives. The explosion was successful, and the Germans were furious. The men were gassed, and the girls were hanged in the presence of the entire camp.

'What do you remember from your arrival in Auschwitz?'

It was in the middle of the night of 17 May 1944. The cattle cars with their human cargo of 3007 Hungarian Jews from Sighet, Transylvania, stopped on a side track, reversed, charged forward again, and paused, only to shortly repeat the procedure. Back and forth we went for several hours, until they finally decided to stop in front of a station that said 'Auschwitz'.

The doors were flung open with a bang, bright floodlights blinded us, and a hellish noise broke out. The roars of SS officers mingled with dogs' barks and children crying. We had to leave the train car as quickly as possible, men to the right, women to the left. Everything we had brought with us had to be left behind. Men in striped clothes with truncheons helped the SS empty the train car. Quickly, quickly, *schnell,*

schnell, they said. Families stood there helpless, not wanting to let go of each other. As truncheons flew through the air and the SS officers falsely reassured us that tomorrow we would be reunited and our luggage delivered, we were all chased down onto the platform.

My father and I lingered behind. Where had we arrived? We could not see any SS officers in the train car, so Papa went to speak to one of the men in striped clothing who looked Jewish. After casting a quick glance around, he whispered: '*Vernichtungslager.*' Extermination camp. At that moment, I realised that Mama had probably sensed what was coming when she said 'they will kill us'.

Under a barrage of barks, insults, and German swearwords, the disoriented, whimpering, and weeping people hurried off the train, trying to avoid a beating. Family members lost each other in the turmoil without a chance to say goodbye. Quick, quick, I too had to jump down onto the platform and stand before my judge. I hopped down from the train car and took a deep breath. After three days in the stuffy, reeking carriage, it was a relief to be able to breathe, even though the air was heavy with a horrific, pungent odour. The floodlights cut through the darkness of the night with hazy brightness. They cast their light upon the anguished crowd, the glistening rails, and the barrels of the SS soldiers' guns.

My mother, flanked on each side by my sister and me, followed the queue of women towards a barbed wire fence, where Dr Mengele, the Nazi doctor who would become infamous for his cruel experiments on Jewish prisoners, stood waiting. With a light flick of his whip, he sent Mama to the right, my sister and me to the left.

That was the night I lost my parents. They were taken to the bathhouse, tricked into believing that they would be taking a shower, but instead of water it was Zyklon B that filled the 'shower cabin'.

I never got to say goodbye to Mama and Papa, never got to hug them one last time.

'What did it mean to have your sister with you in the camps?'

After being separated from our parents, my little sister Livi and I took each other by the hand and started walking. Now, we only had each other. Papa had been taken from us already, in the train car, and now Mama ... I dared not think about what would happen to them. My heart wanted to jump out of my chest; the only person I had to hold on to now was my sister. And I held her hand ever so tightly. I did not yet know how important it was that we had each other. It would become clear as the months went by. From that moment on, we were glued together. We did not let go of each other's hands, one did not move without the other, we slept side by side.

Looking back, it seems like a remarkable transformation to me. Throughout our childhood, we had been like cat and dog. Jealousy blossomed, we fought tooth and nail, and I never wanted her around. But the responsibility of being a big sister hit home in the camp; I was going to defend her with everything I had. On several occasions, however, she would be the one who helped me, even saving my life.

In Auschwitz, many of the other prisoners were jealous of those of us who had each other. People who had been there a long time said that those who were on their own easily lost their will to live. If you were not alone, the responsibility that you felt for each other helped keep the will to live from fading.

It was chance that governed life in the camp. Every day had its surprises. You did not know one day where you would work the next, and after a short time in one labour camp you could be transferred to another. The leadership did not want us to feel too much at home anywhere. They may have been afraid that we would form bonds of friendship that would help us revolt or escape. At such moments, it could easily happen that friends were separated, and that is what happened to Livi and me in Auschwitz, when a working group was put together. I was selected, she was supposed to stay behind. Against all odds, I managed to smuggle myself back to the barracks where she was. Luckily, we were never separated again.

'What was it like to live in the camps?'

Most people are thinking about Auschwitz when they ask this question. But there was a big difference between conditions in the extermination camps and in the labour camps.

The concentration camp is not a German invention, and the Germans were not the only ones to make use of them. The English had camps in India both before and during the war. There, they gathered citizens from enemy countries, for fear of espionage. In those cases, a concentration camp meant an isolated area where those locked up were liberated after the end of the war.

German concentration camps, on the other hand, were built for people who were to be imprisoned indefinitely, due to their ethnicity, religion, or sexual orientation. These people were used and abused, and the ultimate aim was to get rid of them. There were six death camps with gas chambers and crematoriums: Auschwitz, Treblinka, Belzec, Sobibór, Chelmno, and Majdanek. There, killing became an industrial operation: in goes a living human being, out comes ashes. All of these camps were located on formerly Polish or Ukrainian territory. They were extermination camps: the aim was that no one would survive.

Camps like Bergen-Belsen and Theresienstadt had no crematoriums, the prisoners were not gassed. These were not extermination camps, but they were equally inhumane; people died in the thousands of hunger, disease, and maltreatment.

When we ended up in Auschwitz, they had already stripped us of everything we owned, even the clothes on our backs. But we still had the strength to work, and that strength was put to use. The factories needed labour while all the men were at the front, and so a large number of labour camps were set up, spread out across the entire Reich. In these camps, the prisoners had to carry out inhumane work, while suffering maltreatment and scarce food supplies.

But as I mentioned, most people who ask this question want to know what it was like in Auschwitz.

In short, you could say that it was like living in a

grey bubble. The ground was grey with dust, the barracks were grey, the prisoners' clothing was grey, the sky was grey with smoke. It was a life in limbo. Time did not exist, you did not know whether you had been there for a day, a year, all your life ...

I want to quote a survivor, Yehiel De-Nur, who testified at the trial against Adolf Eichmann and said:

> Auschwitz was another planet. Time passed
> on a different scale than here on Earth. No
> children were born there, and no one died
> a natural death. Parents had no children,
> children had no parents.

The purpose of sparing some prisoners from being gassed was to sell them to factories where they would toil away until they had no strength left. The requests came in every so often, and after a selection had been made the chosen ones were transferred to various labour camps adjoining the factories. Those left behind were sent to the gas chambers.

Because the Germans were not intending to keep us alive for long, the food was as might be expected. It was calculated to sustain a human being for just three months. Around 300 grams of black bread, which was mostly sawdust, to last all day, together with 5 grams of margarine and sometimes a dab of jam or slice of sausage. In addition, so-called coffee, a black liquid with only one benefit: it was hot.

In Auschwitz, we were given 'coffee' in the morning and, in the middle of the day, a brown sludge — a soup made from root vegetables and potato peelings, sometimes with a bone in it. In the labour camp, we got 'coffee' in the morning and yet another 'soup' in the evening. Some prisoners were frugal and divided the bread into three, so that it would last for three 'meals'. Others, including myself, could not keep from eating it all as soon as it was doled out.

We lay in our 'bunks', our sleeping quarters, all day, interrupted only by the incessant *Zählappell*, the counting of the prisoners. It was another means of tormenting us. In all weathers, we were chased out to the area in front of the camp, lined up in rows of five, and counted endlessly.

A day could start with us being woken up at the crack of dawn when the block elder, one of the Polish or Czech girls who were in charge of order in the barracks, rushed in roaring *Aufstehen!* — Time to get up! — and turned on the lights. With harsh words, she would hound us out to the latrine. It all had to be quick, the

Zählappell awaited. We stood to attention while they counted us, sometimes for an hour, sometimes several.

The counting went on and on. If you were ill you had to stand there anyway, and if someone had died during the night they put her body out. The block elder had to make sure that the numbers were correct and submit a report to the SS officer. He, in turn, started the control count, and sometimes yet another re-count was needed before the camp commandant arrived. He received the report, and with that we were allowed to return to our barracks. By that time, we were completely exhausted, frozen, and hungry, and we longed for the hot 'coffee' that would only then be handed out.

'Were you always hungry?'

We arrived at Auschwitz after three days without food or water. The fear that held my heart in its iron grip prevented me from noticing how hungry I was. I was an automaton controlled by others, and did exactly as I was told.

Events followed in rapid succession. It all happened so fast that I barely noticed how night gave way to dawn. We stood under a shower; I lapped up its drops greedily.

Next, after we were taken into our barracks, the provisions eventually came, consisting of a piece of black bread each. I was still so shaken by the night's events and the worry for my parents that I could not swallow a single bite. I gave the bread to my sister, and continued to do so over the following days. I only started eating when I realised that if I wanted to survive I could not give away the little I had.

We were never full. Sometimes, the unpalatable bread was not even baked through — it was just black mush. The calories were just enough to keep us from dying, but too little to live on.

When I started eating, my hunger caught up with me. It felt like an empty hole in my stomach that was always gaping. The small piece of bread could not fill it, instead it aroused a demand for more. The days went by, and the hunger tore at my bowels. It was a collective hunger; us girls were one single craving belly. All we ever talked about was different ways to trick our hunger.

Later, when we ended up in the labour camps, the hunger had become familiar. We were used to it. The constant hungry feeling became something that was simply there. Every now and then, my stomach would revolt and begin to hurt, but when that happened I chewed saliva to trick it into thinking I was eating. You could also trick your stomach by talking about cooking, recipes, and dishes until the dribble started flowing. My last thought before I went out like a light in the evening was often of the small piece of bread that I would get in the morning. It soothed my hunger for the time being, at least.

We were always on the lookout for something edible. A few girls worked in the kitchen, and it was important to be friends with them. They sometimes managed to smuggle out potatoes or a piece of bread to cheer up a friend. Joy also came from marching to work along the vegetable fields, where I would brave the risk of a beating to steal one or two stalks of broccoli.

The hunger was stronger than the fear of punishment.

Only once was I allowed to eat until I was full.

Our group was clearing up after the bombing of an oil depot. When the lunch signal came and our watery soup was supposed to arrive, we were taken into a canteen instead. The tables were set, crowned in the middle by a large bread basket. I did not dare to even think about touching the bread until the guard insisted. To my great astonishment, we were allowed to eat as much as we wanted. When the basket was empty, we got another one. It was difficult to fathom what was happening, it felt like velvet over my aching tummy. I ate, and ate, and ate. I was happy. I had never understood that bread could make you happy. Ever since, I feel an almost religious reverence for bread and potatoes. No meal is a meal for me without bread.

The joy quickly passed. Someone must have made a mistake. It would only be a one-time occurrence, and retribution for that day's satisfaction was exacted through even more intense feelings of hunger over the following days as our stomachs shrunk back. We simply had to keep swallowing and trying to imagine that we were not hungry.

We went on like this until we were freed. When the British troops found us, hollow-eyed and emaciated, they wanted to help, and shared with us some of their rich, canned soldier's food. Most of us devoured it; no one knew that it was lethal, that we would not be able to digest it. As luck would have it, I was not tempted. If someone had offered me a can, I would probably have eaten it. I was lucky that, instead, I met someone who offered me two raw potatoes.

'What languages were spoken in Auschwitz?'

Auschwitz was a Tower of Babel where all European languages could be heard. But the ruling language was of course German, and if you did not know it you were in trouble.

It was worst for the Italians, very few of whom spoke any German. The SS did not accept that some of us did not understand their language, and took it for disobedience when an order was not carried out. I remember a small and slender Greek woman from Rhodes who spoke of the beating she got when she did not understand what was asked of her. Those who did not understand the words of command did not live long, and many Greeks and Italians paid with their lives.

The Eastern European Jews had an advantage. Because they spoke Yiddish, they usually understood what was asked of them and were therefore not as vulnerable as the Italians. I myself had a passive knowledge of Yiddish, as my parents spoke it when they did not want us children to understand them. What's more, I had studied some German at school. It put me in a favourable position.

In the vast Auschwitz-Birkenau, the prisoners were segregated based on nationality, so I did not have many opportunities to hear all the spoken languages. The only place where you could meet others from different blocks was by the latrine. There, I tried to exchange a few words with other girls.

In addition to the Greek woman, I also met Rose, a small Dutch girl. She spoke German, but I found it difficult to understand her as she had the Dutch, guttural R. Luckily, it did not prevent the SS soldiers from understanding her, and she talked about her appointment as *Blockova* (responsible for order in the barracks) and its associated benefits, such as better food, better clothing, and more liberties.

'What helped you to survive?'

Many people do not believe in chance, but if I am to answer the question of what helped me to survive, it is all that I can point to. Without chance, nothing could have helped. There was no logic in the camp; you never knew where to be, or not to be, in order to survive. You might be killed by an SS officer doing target practice just for the fun of it. A kindness could mean death; Dr Mengele, for example, was known for giving out sweets to the children he would then torture with his experiments.

'How did you cope?' many students say to me. 'I would have died.'

You may think so, but dying is not easy. It can be difficult to live, but it is all that we know, and we cling to life until the very end.

Many nights, after a hard day's work, I thought that

I could not go on for another day. But when I woke up, I was once again the obedient lamb that carried out the same tasks as yesterday, in the hope that, as long as I did as they said, they would not shoot me. While there is life in us, we want to go on living, no matter what happens. Many of us were tortured, and still did not give up. I hope that I too would have clung to life in that situation, but you never know what you will do.

In Auschwitz, I sometimes thought in despair: 'Not one more day, tomorrow I will throw myself on the electric barbed wire.' But then came the next thought: 'This would do the Nazis' work for them. It is, after all, what they want: to get rid of us.'

What helped guard against these gloomy thoughts was having my sister with me. We felt responsible for each other, there was a meaning to the meaninglessness. If she was downhearted, I tried to cheer her up. If I was sad, she joked around. We would probably not have survived without each other.

The solidarity, the circle of friends from my block, also meant a great deal. In the evenings, we sat around trying to dispel the bad thoughts with old and new stories, poems, and recipes. We tried to quell our hunger by 'cooking', explaining in detail how certain dishes should be prepared, until we could almost smell the stuffed cabbage rolls and taste the meatballs.

There were some other things that were also crucial to the survival of those of us from Hungary. Above all, the fact that we were not taken prisoner until the spring of 1944. It meant that we spent barely a year in the camp, unlike those who had to suffer for much longer.

The thought that we must survive in order to tell of everything that had happened to us after the war was often in our minds. At the same time, we doubted that anyone would want to listen.

'Was there solidarity in the camp?'

You might think that our shared fate would have brought us together. But the truth is that the solidarity was not what it could have been.

As often happens when a group ends up together, in-groups and out-groups formed. Girls who came from the same country stuck together, past prejudices prevailed, Polish-Jewish girls considered themselves better than the Hungarians, and the Hungarians thought themselves superior to the Polish. Within the Hungarian group, coteries also formed, as those who came from the same towns stuck together.

Those who came from the same area, perhaps on the same train, helped each other the best they could. If someone from the group had been given a role, such as working in the kitchen, that could give the others an opportunity for larger portions, for example. The girls shared their benefits with their group, and made sure that 'their' girls were prioritised. When food was given out it was of great importance to get the soup from the bottom of the pot. That was where the vegetables were, sometimes even a scrap of meat. We queued for the soup and glared jealously at the swinging of the ladle. Has it plunged far enough down, or will it be only water today? The block elder wanted to seem fair, so did not look at who was in line — the ladle was supposed to sink as deeply for everyone. But she knew where her pack was, if they were first, in the middle, or last. And then the ladle plunged properly.

The desire to stay alive was so strong that people would steal bread from their kin: daughter from mother, sister from sister. The opposite also happened, but more rarely. In my group, there was a woman who had previously been known as mean and selfish. Now, she showed herself to be self-sacrificing and generous, she helped where she could and gave up her own benefits when someone else was in greater need.

Denunciation was not rare. In order to enjoy some advantage, there were those who would inform on their friends. It happened to me. I was one of the few who knew German, and I was taller than the others, so when we were sent to work in Eidelstedt, I was appointed *kapo*. To be *kapo* meant being the extended arm of the SS, and making sure that the group worked hard. For this you were rewarded with an extra bowl of soup. You could not turn down the appointment, but you could sabotage the job.

After a short march to work, we arrived at a factory in ruins, where we had to clear up among the rubble. We were supposed to form a chain and pass bricks to the other side, to be placed in neat piles. My task was to ensure the girls were efficient, but I started by placing a lookout whose job it was to alert us when an SS guard approached. The girls could take it easy until the look-out gave warning, and then put their backs into it.

No more than two days passed before I was reported by one of the Polish girls. One bowl of soup meant that much to her.

'What was it like to be a woman in the camps?'

When it came to the treatment of prisoners, little difference was made between women and men. Women were not spared the heavy work and we were punished just as harshly. To the SS men, we were not women; we were objects who would carry out their orders.

Women, especially the young, tried to keep their womanliness, even in insufferable conditions. When we came to the labour camp and met French prisoners-of-war on the same worksite, we searched among the ruins for lipstick or creams. Our vanity was awoken, and we wanted to make ourselves attractive to these handsome young men. Innocent little romances flared up, soon every girl had 'her own' Frenchman.

We were strictly prohibited from communicating with each other, but in unsupervised moments the

Frenchman would 'drop' a small gift before 'his' girl as she passed by, who, in turn, 'dropped' a letter with a few words of thanks. We had to be careful that no SS soldier was nearby when it happened; such things would lead to harsh punishments. Harsh punishments would also be the consequence if women and men were caught together, but from what I remember it never happened in any of the labour camps I was in. It did happen in Auschwitz, however.

In Auschwitz, we lived in large barracks, around 500 in each. We were supervised by a Polish girl, Itka, who was the block elder. As help, she had her sister, Elsa. These girls came from Poland, had already been in Auschwitz for a couple of years, and were beautiful and well fed. As extra perks, they were allowed to keep their lovely hair, they wore civilian clothes, and they were given more food.

One day, we could not find Elsa, and when she appeared she was shaven and puffy-eyed. We wondered what had happened, and eventually we got it out of her. A man who worked in the task force at the crematoriums visited the girls in secret, and provided them with some extra necessities. Naturally, sexual feelings also arose; Elsa fell in love. I do not know how long it went on for, but one day they were caught by an SS soldier.

She was beaten, her hair was shaved off, and she was stripped of all her perks. The man was beaten too, and most likely did not survive.

'What was it like to have your period?'

The women packed their menstrual pads before departure, not suspecting that they would be allowed to keep neither the pads nor any other possessions. As it turned out, however, we would not have had any use for them anyway. Menstruation happened perhaps once or twice, and on those occasions we were miserable, of course. There was nothing to collect the blood with. If we were lucky, we were given a rag by the block elder, the girl who was supervising us. Risking punishment, we sometimes dared to tear off a piece from our dress, but usually we had to walk around with bloody clothes, the blood running down our legs. It was important not to find yourself before an SS man, he would shower us with insults — *dreckige Judesau*, filthy Jewish pig who can't keep clean — and beat us black and blue.

One day, my friend Dora noticed that she should have had her period three days previously. She thought that it was strange; after all, she had not been with anyone. More and more of us made the same discovery; only a few got their bleeding during the weeks after our arrival. Some thought that they were with child, but soon we all understood that it was not a sign of pregnancy. Menstruation simply stopped. There was a rumour that it was caused by a bromine additive in the bread, but this has never been confirmed. It is true that menstruation can cease due to a poor diet, as is the case for people with anorexia, but that could not have been the explanation here — we stopped getting our periods too soon after our arrival to Auschwitz. We must have been given something that affected our hormones.

We were afraid that we would never get our periods again, that we would not be able to have children. Luckily, that is not what happened. We regained our regular cycles when our diets returned to normal. After the war, however, some women decided not to have children, out of fear that everything they had been through could happen again. Later, when they became old, some of them regretted not having a family. They felt very lonely.

'Were you raped?'

Wartime rape has always been used as a way for one side to violate what is perceived as the other's property, its women. Not so in Germany. In Nazi Germany, rape was, in principle, banned, as interracial relations were forbidden by law. In practice, however, things were different.

Luckily, no one in our group was subjected to rape, and for a long time I was not aware that it had happened elsewhere in the camps. It was not until after the war that I found out. I met girls who had dreadful stories to tell.

In order to maintain morale among the SS soldiers, brothels were established — nicer ones for the officers, and more basic for the soldiers. Jewish girls were sent there, and if you wanted to stay alive you had to obey. After a day's hard labour at the worksite, a beautiful girl could be picked up in the evening and taken to the brothel, only to be returned to work the following morning.

Others had to serve there around the clock. These girls did not last long. There were, however, fortunate girls who could use their womanliness to make a soldier fall in love with them. A girl in this position could have a fairly decent life alongside her protective soldier, especially if he was high in the pecking order.

A high-ranking SS officer could choose a girl to run his household, and she would be excused from the hard labour outside. But even in those cases there was no guarantee that the girl would survive in the uncertain, irrational world of Nazism.

'Were you afraid of death?'

Death was not something that I was afraid of. What felt worse was the uncertainty, the endless waiting, the anxiety. The anxiety never let up. It was like a humming in the background, and would only give way when a sharper, more acute fear set in.

What I was afraid of was *how* death would come. Ceasing to exist was our greatest wish, but it was the road there that frightened us. The studied cruelty of the Nazis could cause much pain before death arrived. That was what I feared.

I remember wondering in the morning when I woke up: 'Will I make it through the day?' But there was no time to meditate. The yells and blows of the SS officers made me leap out of bed and set about dealing with the prescribed agenda: 'making' the straw bed, visiting the latrine, and then lining up to be counted. The march to work followed, and it was not until I got back into bed at night that I had the strength to think.

I usually ended the day by remembering a poem by the Hungarian poet János Arany, which, in amateur translation, goes roughly like this:

> Thank you, God
> for evening's return
> The suffering Earth
> now rests peacefully.

'How were you dressed?'

When we arrived at Auschwitz we had to strip naked. We put all of our clothes in one pile, our shoes tied together in another. I wondered quietly how everyone would find their own clothes again.

It was only later that I found out that the clothes were going to be sent to Germany, once a task force had separated out the worst items. What was not sent off would be washed and sterilised, and — painted with a yellow cross — used as prison clothes. In exchange, we were given grey tunics of varying length and ill-shaped underwear in a coarse fabric.

I cannot remember whether we were given socks, but we did get a handkerchief, which we used to cover our shaved heads.

When we were selected for work, we got to change into 'civilian' clothes with a yellow cross painted on our dresses so we would not be confused with those who were to remain behind. These clothes were also exchanged sometimes. When the cold set in, we were given an additional, so-called 'warmer' piece of clothing.

I was given a coat, albeit very light, while my sister Livi got a cardigan. It had originally belonged to her favourite cousin, Ditsi. That is how we realised that she too had walked under *'Arbeit macht frei'*, the cynical sign that hung above the entrance to Auschwitz. The 'warm' clothes had to be returned in the spring, the others we kept until liberation.

After liberation, we wanted to get rid of these clothes as quickly as possible and get new ones, and we managed this in many different ways. Sometimes, we received gifts from the British soldiers, or else we went out into the neighbourhood and searched. We could 'find' clothes drying on a clothesline, which we unscrupulously acquired — after all, the Germans had taken so much more from us. It was not called theft, it was called 'organising'. Girls who were good at sewing were at a premium. Blankets and sheets transformed under their nimble fingers. They turned into skirts, jackets, and dresses.

I, myself, had a dress made from a green curtain, and 'found' a pair of blue sailor's trousers made from wool. I wore the trousers when we travelled to Sweden. In Lübeck, we and our clothes were sterilised, and the girls who had wearable clothes got to keep them. I wore the trousers to my first job in Stockholm.

With my first paycheque, I bought a black woollen dress that cost me my entire month's salary, 100 kronor. It was worth the price. Finally, I could put on something 'elegant', that gave me confidence when I met up with friends at a café on a Sunday afternoon.

'Did you get ill?'

It was important not to fall ill. We would only survive for as long as we could work, and were we to become ill they would have no use for us. We knew that if we were deemed useless, the gas chamber awaited. As a result, we were rarely seriously ill. Those of us who had previously suffered from chronic pain were suddenly free of it. No constant headache, no stomach ulcers. We sometimes had lesser ailments, and when that happened we had to visit the *Revier*, as the infirmary was called. The nurse was one of the prisoners, and she did not have much to relieve our suffering with. The same ointment, Ichthyol, was used both for sore throats and for boils. The only relief such a visit could bring was a moment's rest and a few soothing words.

If anyone had a fever or was so ill that she could not work, us girls tried to protect her. We carried out her work and let her rest in a corner, while someone made sure that no SS guard discovered her. Sometimes a kind foreman would let her sit in his work shed, and would defend her to any potential SS visitors by saying that the girl was helping him with his indoors work. If the guard was in a good mood, he might let her stay, otherwise he would chase her out.

The *Revier* had a number of beds, so the sick could stay there instead of going out into the icy cold. The reason we were so afraid of staying was that you never knew when the SS doctor's visit might happen. When he came, the sick had to be lined up naked for examination, and being too thin was enough of a reason to be sentenced to death.

The nurse, who wanted to save the girls, could not do much. However, I do know of one case in which she hid a gravely ill, unconscious girl so skilfully that she was not discovered. The girl eventually recovered and left the *Revier*.

Another interesting case was when an SS doctor became smitten with a beautiful girl, and instead of giving her a death sentence he transferred her to the soldiers' *Revier*. What happened after, I do not know; I never saw her again.

I, myself, visited the *Revier* a few times, when the

rough clogs and the cold caused big boils to grow on my feet. I do not know whether it was the notorious wonder ointment or the fact that spring was in the air, but the boils went away with time.

'Were there kind SS soldiers?'

I never met an SS soldier who was kind. At best, our guards were completely disinterested. They were simply doing their job, and if the job called for a beating they would use their truncheons. Some were known for being particularly mean, some were 'just' mean, and any of them could strike you for no reason. You could not say that I experienced any real kindness. The SS soldiers were trained to be brutal and cold.

In Himmler's infamous and often-quoted speech, he praises the brutality of those who shot Jews: 'To have endured this and remained decent, that has made us hard. This is a glorious page in our history ...' In his 1926 book *Die zweite revolution* Goebbels said: 'We will only reach our goal when we are brave enough to laugh as we destroy and ruin that which was once holy to us, such as tradition, education, friendship, and human affection.'

Those who worked in the SS — like all of us — had both good and evil inside them, but they chose evil. Afterwards, many argued that they only fired shots because they had to. However, research has shown that this was not always the case. In his book *Ordinary Men*, the historian Christopher Browning has pointed out that only a few fell out of line despite being told that they would be excused if their conscience would not allow them to kill. Instead of choosing for themselves, the men gave in to peer pressure. Likewise, decent Germans also chose evil under certain circumstances. We all have a choice.

Our guards were young SS soldiers, men and women who had sworn a solemn oath to dutifully obey and protect the Führer, to live and die for him. Their Nazi upbringing began at an early age, when they were at their most malleable. On a few occasions, the guards were from the *Wehrmacht*. These were soldiers from the regular army, older men who had been drafted. There was a big difference between the two groups; the latter were gentler, their minds had not yet been brainwashed.

One day as we were walking to our work site, we were not accompanied by young SS soldiers with truncheons, but by soldiers from the *Wehrmacht* who carried rifles over their backs. It was the first and only time that the guards spoke *with* us, not simply barking their commands *at* us. One of these soldiers, Herman, seemed curious, and since I was one of the few who spoke German he walked by my side as we marched in rows of five. He started talking to me, asking me who I was and where I came from. He told me a little about some of his own difficulties at home. It turned out that he had a daughter who was my age, and perhaps that is why he sought me out on those few occasions when the *Wehrmacht* stayed at the camp. Sometimes he brought me an apple, or a potato. But they had little food, too. His friendly spirit was a ray of sunshine in the darkness that enveloped me. It only lasted for a very brief time, however. Soon, the regular SS lads were back, those who hit us without mercy if someone dropped behind or fell out of line.

Sometimes, we passed by fields where vegetables had recently been harvested: Brussels sprouts, broccoli, and more. Whenever we saw a few stalks still shooting up through the mud, we rushed over to pull them up, despite the risk of getting a beating. It meant a precious addition to that day's poor ration. Especially for the sick girls, who still dragged themselves off to work.

Elisabet, a beautiful Hungarian-Jewish girl, became

very ill, lost consciousness, and was taken to the infirmary. The next day, the SS doctor came by, stopped by every sickbed, and let the nurse know his verdict with a nod of his head. At Elisabet's bed, he asked about her illness. He addressed her kindly with the words 'And you, young girl, what ails you?'

She answered: 'I ache all over, but I'm not so young, I have already studied medicine.'

The SS doctor then gave the order that she should be taken to another barracks, and there she actually returned to health.

The same person who felt no pangs of conscience when sending someone to their death saved another's life. We sometimes meet this same duplicity in the rest of society.

Another day, my friend Lilly fell unconscious, and to our great sorrow she was taken to the *Revier*. When the days went by and she did not return, we thought we would never see her again. But all of a sudden, she was standing there during *Zählappell*, the prisoner count.

When we asked what had happened, she said that she had vague memories of being hidden in some cubbyhole every time an SS doctor came by for a check-up. The staff in the *Revier* were our fellow prisoners, and SS cruelties could sometimes be balanced out by solidarity.

Sara, one of my fellow prisoners from Poland, told me that before her internment she had hidden in a place she believed to be safe. However, she had to initiate someone into her plans so that her husband could find her. She chose their neighbour N, who had always been kind to them. The next day, the police came for her, and that is when she understood that the neighbour's kindness had its limits.

Today, I often think about how I would have acted if I, born in 1924 in Sighet, had seen the light of day as a German child in Berlin instead. I, too, would surely have received my share of brainwashing in *Bund Deutscher Mädel*, the association for girls that corresponded to the boys' *Hitlerjugend*.

Perhaps I would have become a female SS guard. They were no better than the male ones. How would I have acted? Would I have beaten the prisoners? Saved them? If I had parents with a moral strength whose upbringing could have counteracted *BDM*, perhaps I would have shown mercy. One can only hope. If a person knows that she has a choice, there is an opportunity to choose good over evil.

I can, however, tell you how 12-year-old Noa reacted. He lived in a ghetto in Poland, where hunger was spreading. Everyone was trying to find something to eat, through either bartering or theft. The children were the most skilful. They snuck out of the ghetto with something they could trade for food. They often managed to return with some potatoes or turnips.

One day, Noa was caught by an SS man who wanted to know who the brains behind these 'outings' was. Noa refused to answer the question. The SS man tempted him by saying that he would get to keep the potato, and get another one, and that he would be appointed to the ghetto police. The ghetto police received extra benefits and, relatively, plenty of food, while the ghetto inhabitants starved. Noa steadfastly refused to become the SS man's informant, even though he knew that he would be beaten for his insubordination.

'Did you dream at night?'

Spontaneously, I would say no. But things were not always the same, everything changed depending on where we were.

In Auschwitz, we slept the short hours we were allowed as if we had been knocked out cold with a brick. Heavy and dreamless, it was a sleep that offered no rest.

In the labour camps, things were different. Though our sleeping hours were not longer, the dreams started coming. Usually, we dreamed that we were at home within the family circle, and waking up was very painful. I dreamed that I was taking a stroll in a sunny meadow, hand in hand with my father, and he was just telling me a story when the sharp wake-up light was turned on and Papa's voice was exchanged for the harsh German *Aufwachen*, get up, *schnell*, quickly, *raus, raus*, out, out ...

I tried to imagine that it was the dream that was reality, and that the daily toil was just a bad nightmare ... I tried to keep my balance in the harsh reality with the help of my imagination.

'What was the best?'

The best? Could anything have been the best? When I got this question, I was confounded. Nothing was good, but there were moments when we could forget where we were and even laugh.

It felt good at night, when the day's toil was over, when we could stretch our tired limbs out on the hard bunk. We had survived. I knew that the night would be very short, and it would not offer much rest, but in the moment it felt good.

Before bedtime, the group of friends sat huddled together on one of the beds, and held a 'literary salon'. We recited poems, read stories, and shared memories, or 'cooked', exchanged recipes, talked about the delicious dishes we longed for.

I had a special experience in Auschwitz that offered some light in the blackness of our existence. One morning, an SS man entered the barracks and asked for two volunteers for some work. My friend Olga and I put ourselves forward. The soldier, who carried a rifle over his back, took us away. We passed by one area after another surrounded by barbed wire fence, until we came to one with smaller barracks. These were the soldiers' barracks, and we were tasked with cleaning and scrubbing the floors.

As we approached the barracks, a lush, verdant birch tree caught my attention. It was like a mirage, to see such greenery after the greyness of Auschwitz. There was life outside, everything was not lost.

Olga and I just looked, first at the tree, then at each other, and without speaking we knew what the other was thinking. We would smuggle some leaves into the camp, so that everyone else could see it too. The soldier hurried us on, we were to enter the barracks and get to work. He gave us instructions, a bucket of cold water, and a rag.

It turned into a hard day's work. In order to get the very dirty floors into a somewhat clean state, we needed to gather a few branches. Under the soldier's goading insults, we toiled away with the branches, using our knuckles and nails to make the floor a little less grubby.

When the signal came for the end of the working

day, we could breathe again. '*Feierabend*', the soldier said when evening came, 'Time to call it a day'. We were to return to the camp, where the counting of the prisoners awaited. I managed to tear off a few leaves, but on the way home I was very tense: would I be able to smuggle them inside, or would we be searched? Bringing in as much as a blade of grass was strictly prohibited. I hid a branch in the hem of my dress and put a leaf in my mouth. So did Olga. Trembling, we walked past the gatekeeper and — we made it.

Our legs shook as we waited for the counting to end. Later, when we entered the barracks and presented the leaves, there was much joy. A hope arose in all of our friends that a brighter future would be waiting outside, even for us.

'When did you realise that there was a genocide happening?'

During the Second World War, the word 'genocide' did not exist, neither in my own nor in anyone else's vocabulary. It only became clear to me that widespread killing was taking place when I found myself in Auschwitz. Before that, not many understood that this was not just the killing of certain individuals, that it encompassed an entire people who were to be wiped off the face of the earth.

'How did you picture your life after the war?'

I was very naïve. That the Germans would lose the war, I was sure of, but I did not understand that everything could not go back to how it had been before. I was utterly convinced that after the war Transylvania would once again become part of Romania. Those early teenage dreams still lingered in my mind. I would return, study medicine, and train as a paediatrician. I would go to Africa and heal the sick.

I could not imagine that, even if the Allies won, nothing would be as it once was.

Had we not studied history in school? Yes, we had, but that was mostly dates and years, names of rulers and battlefields, a kind of learning that did not move us and was soon forgotten. I was not prepared. I did not understand that life could not go on as before.

'How did you picture your life after the war?'

With all the effort in the world, I would never have been able to foresee what awaited us after the war.

'What happened to your sister?'

Livi saved my life in Bergen-Belsen. During the commotion after liberation, I ran a high fever and fell unconscious. She found a doctor among the liberated prisoners, who seemed to be in need of a doctor himself. I remember his face, when he said, 'Yes, you are sick, and many of the sick die here.' I understood then that I too would die. I submitted to my fate, closed my eyes, and after that I remember nothing more until my sister stood by my bedside, and I understood that I needed to learn to walk again. I had been unconscious for several weeks, and Livi had helped nurse me back to life.

In the summer of 1945, we came to Sweden, and here we both stayed. Livi married young, she was just 17 years old when she met her Hans, who was 27. He was also just a child when he'd had to leave his parents in Germany to save himself. He came to Denmark, and from there to Sweden, with the Danish rescue action. They had their first child when Livi was 19, and then another two. He was taken ill with Alzheimer's disease and died in 2000.

Nowadays, Livi and I live close to each other. When we were younger, we saw each other every day. Today, we both have difficulty walking, so we speak on the phone instead. Every morning around nine o'clock, one of us calls, and we see each other as often as possible. She is approaching her nineties, though she still visits schools to talk about our life stories.

'How many people from your hometown survived the war?'

That is a question that cannot be answered. Those who survived spread to the ends of the world. There were not many who returned.

We were 3007 men, women, and children who were loaded onto the train on the morning of 15 May 1944. When our group of women was counted after the selection, on the night we arrived in Auschwitz, 17 May, there were 486 of us. The number of men could have been similar. If we suppose that the same was true for the subsequent five trains, it means that a third survived the initial selection. How many of them died later, no one knows.

In my own family, 10 of the 31 who lived in Sighet survived. Those who wanted to return faced great difficulties. There was no functioning transport network after the war, so most people walked on foot, hitched a ride in a car, or jumped on board a train when they happened upon one.

Sanyi, my father's youngest brother, made it. He had worked in a bakery in Auschwitz, and so had had access to bread. He hoped to find his wife Helen, and when the war was over he set out for Sighet on foot. Then something incredible happened. When he had made it as far as to Prague, and was just walking around in the streets, he suddenly ran into Helen. She, too, had been freed from a labour camp and was on her way to Sighet, hoping to find her husband.

It was one of few happy reunions; most people found no one when they finally reached Sighet. In many cases, not even their houses remained. Sanyi and Helen were lucky once more; their house was intact, and they could move in and start a new life. They did not stay long, however. Sighet had been liberated by the Russians in the autumn of 1944, and now the population lived under a strict communist regime. Sanyi and Helen left Romania as soon as possible, and finally settled in Los Angeles.

'Were you jubilant when you were liberated?'

We were liberated while the war was still raging. British troops on their way to Berlin liberated us from Bergen-Belsen on 15 April 1945. You may think that I would have been jubilant, but I was so weakened and apathetic that I could barely feel joy. My only thought was that the next day I would go to the men's camp and start looking for my father. It was a long time before I could cheer for freedom.

I was glad, of course, but cheering requires strength, and that took time.

The first time I felt jubilant was after we had reached Sweden, when my sister and I were walking across Västerbron, a bridge in Stockholm built on two large arches with a panoramic view of the city. When I looked behind me, there were no SS soldiers. I heard no dogs barking, and all I saw were peaceful Swedish families on tandem bikes enjoying their Sunday in the sunshine. Livi and I were thinking the same thing. We looked at each other and started dancing in the middle of the bridge.

'Why did you choose Sweden?'

I usually say that Sweden chose me. Just before the end of the war, when the Germans understood that defeat was near, everything and everyone who could bear witness to their crimes had to be destroyed. They needed to empty the camps and get rid of their inhabitants somehow. At the time, we — my sister Livi and I — were in Eidelstedt, a labour camp near Hamburg.

One day at the beginning of April, we received orders to gather in one of the rooms in the barracks, all 200 of us together. The instruction was enough to scare us; change was never good. But it was nothing compared to what followed. The SS woman 'fat Anna', as we called the mean *Aufseherin*, ordered us to strip naked. 'Where you're going, you'll need no clothes,' she added. We took our clothes off and sat there for a good while, trembling with both cold and fear. After a while,

Schara, the camp commandant, came by, looked at us with bewilderment, and asked why we were sitting there naked. When he heard that we were following Anna's orders, he gave her a displeased look and had us quickly put our clothes back on again. We could breathe a little easier, but still did not know what it was all about; we were still scared. Dressed, we were taken to the train station, and with a sense of *déjà vu* we were once again put in a cattle car with two buckets of water and two buckets to relieve ourselves in. No food. Where were we going? Back to Auschwitz? By then, Auschwitz had been liberated, but we did not know that.

The train crawled along at a snail's pace for three days and three nights. It charged forward, stopped, waited on a side track while military transports passed, and chuffed off again. One night, while we were standing still, we could hear the rattle of a door opening and the sound of a gunshot. Now, we were fully convinced that our final moment had come, we would all be executed. I waited tensely for the next shot. Soon, the door to our train car would be opened, it would be our turn.

Transformed into a statue, I squeezed my sister's hand and held my breath. But nothing happened, one minute passed, two, three, five, and I began to breathe again. I never found out who was shot and why, but after a few hours the train started moving again, and after some time we were dumped by a field with an area surrounded by a barbed wire fence. A woman stood by the gate and I asked her where we had arrived. Bergen-Belsen, she said, and added laconically: 'There is work, there is no bread, there is no gas.' I was a little relieved and thought: 'I still have the strength to work, perhaps I will last for a time without bread. The most important thing is that there is no gas.' Afterwards, I worked out that it must have been 7 April 1945.

We were housed in clean barracks. Only after liberation did I understand how lucky we'd been, when I saw the inside of the other barracks, riddled with lice. A group of prominent Jews had been kept there before us, awaiting exchange with German prisoners-of-war. We had actually met them when we arrived; they had been on their way to the train.

It was not just bread that was missing, there was no water either. We have the so-called coffee to thank for our survival, the black liquid we were served twice a day. We lay on our bunks, growing increasingly weak, completely apathetic, and simply waited for death, when there was suddenly a hustle and bustle outside. It turned out that British soldiers on their way to Berlin had stumbled upon our camp, and decided to enter and liberate us. It was 15 April 1945.

I only have hazy recollections of what happened afterwards. What I remember is that I became gravely ill. It was typhoid that I had picked up while I had been running around the camp looking for Papa. Livi took care of me, and I have her to thank for saving my life. A couple of months later, a Swedish delegation came to Bergen-Belsen with a mission to bring 10,000 survivors to Sweden for six months' convalescence. Livi and I were among them. After a train journey and disinfection in Lübeck, we were put on an ambulance boat with the destination Malmö, Sweden. I will never forget that journey, that feeling of freedom.

'How were you received in Sweden?'

The boat that took us to Sweden was called *Rönnskär* and was a cargo boat that had been converted into ambulance transport. It was a new experience for me — I had never travelled by boat, never seen the sea. We were not allowed to be on deck during the day, the war was not yet over and the North Sea was riddled with mines. Pilot boats scouted out a route forward, and we had to stay moored at night. That is when I was allowed to go upstairs, breathe the sea air, and enjoy the panoramic view. I relished the journey.

Our expectations were high. My fellow passengers and I felt that we had been chosen for a new life, where we would be treated as special guests and all of our needs would be satisfied. Our beds on the boat were made with paper sheets, and their rustling at my slightest movement made me feel special, like a praline wrapped in silver tissue. Three days and three nights passed quickly, and we were joyous when we arrived in Malmö. We were met by *lottor*, members of the women's wing of the Swedish Home Guard, who brought us cocoa and sandwiches. We thought that we had ended up in paradise, and could not get enough of the sandwiches and that heavenly drink, cocoa. For me, ever since then cocoa has been the very emblem of the good life in Sweden.

From the port, we were driven by tram to the Linnaeus School, where we were to be housed. What I remember most from that time is the food. The good food, horseradish beef, and the strange food, black pudding with little hats of lingonberries, which went down fine nonetheless. We ate and ate, and were never full. The food was the bright spot in our lives, and we thoroughly enjoyed it. We were served five meals a day, but were always afraid that we would run out. Most of us took food from the dining hall and hid it under our pillows. The fact that we were allowed to get sandwiches between meals did not stop us, nor did the patient staff's assurances that there would always be more food. This insatiable hunger affected us for the rest of our lives in different ways: some of us became anorexic, but most of us have, ever since then, kept an overstocked fridge.

The locals gathered outside the school fence to peek at the survivors from Bergen-Belsen, but we were forbidden from approaching them. We were kept in quarantine for six weeks, and only then were we allowed to acquaint ourselves with the Swedes outside. They were kind and curious, some brought small gifts, but they did not really want to hear our stories. We were well received; it was not yet an opportune time for people to show their prejudice, their Nazi leanings, their anti-Semitism. All of this was swept under the rug. Not until the 1980s did Nazism begin to surface again, to spread once more. When I think about it, I can see this pattern today, too. People are empathetic; they want to help, to share their abundance, but as soon as it becomes a matter of making sacrifices, sharing in the narrower sense, or giving up one's time, it becomes more difficult.

We felt welcome in Sweden. When the initial euphoria had settled and we experienced our first setbacks, we began to think about leaving the country. But slowly we got used to Sweden, and Sweden got used to us. We learnt that there is no paradise on earth. In Sweden, like in other countries, some things are good, others bad. So now, I feel at home.

'How did you deal with your trauma?'

I had the luck of being able to come to Sweden as early as the summer of 1945. It was a difficult time. I was tormented by having lost my entire family except for my sister. I was tortured by thoughts of how my parents had been murdered while I had survived. How many could still be alive out of the 56 people in my extended family?

The word 'trauma' was barely known, and no one had heard of 'trauma processing'. The notion that a person can suffer from lasting trauma was only brought to attention when more and more survivors complained of health problems. Already during the First World War, some soldiers suffered as a result of what they had been subjected to, but for a long time this suffering was not accepted as a mental disorder. It was called 'shell shock', and the soldiers were sent back to the front. When the symptoms returned, they were accused of being malingerers.

When more and more survivors went to see the doctor, and the latter could not find any physical explanation for their symptoms, the notion that the problems could be of a mental nature, a result of their wartime experiences, began to take root. It took a number of years, but slowly the realisation came that only processing can help those who suffer. A number of trauma centres were set up, and the refugees who came later were given the opportunity to process their experiences.

I was lucky. I had a good constitution, was athletic, fairly strong, and had a stubborn will. Apparently, I also had good genes. In addition to these qualities, during my early childhood, which can nurture or deprive an individual of safety, trust, and confidence, I was lucky to have had devoted and perceptive parents, providing me with a strong start to my life's journey. I had a loving mother and a father who was present. The first three months leave their mark on the individual, according to psychologists. That is when the child sees its own reflection in its mother's eyes, and finds affirmation of being welcome in the world. This security was what helped me after the war, on the path back to life.

Moreover, I had instinctively begun to process my experiences by writing a diary. I had been keeping a diary ever since my early teens, and now I did so again. It became a kind of self-analysis. Marianne, a Swedish girl my age who became my friend, supported me; she meant a great deal to me. She became like an older sister. She taught me to make a 'balance sheet', to note down everything that was good on one side of a paper, and everything I had lost on the opposite. It did not help then, but with time it became useful.

At the same time, I wanted to be strong in front of Livi. While Marianne became like an older sister, I felt that I had to support my younger sister. It was a painful time, and the pain did not ease until I started working, and even then only some of the time. Work required all my concentration during the day, but in the evenings, the questions that tormented me would resurface. What was the purpose of it all, why had *I* survived? I had a hard time finding the answer, but knew there must be a reason that I was still alive. And then one day, it revealed itself to me.

'What made you start lecturing?'

I finally realised that I had survived so that someone could tell of what happened during the Holocaust. If no one tells the story of the Holocaust, it will be forgotten, and what is forgotten may easily be repeated. If it fades into oblivion, no one will remember that six million Jews, and countless communists, gay people, people with disabilities, Roma, and others — considered to be of less than human value — ever existed.

The first time I realised this was when a teacher called and asked me to speak at her school.

When I retired, in the beginning of the 1980s, I started writing books about what had happened. The first was *Fragments of a Life: the road to Auschwitz* (translated into English by Michael Meyer).

Since then, I have lectured for many years, and I

have done so for two reasons: so that the names of my parents, Frida Klein Szmuk and Ignatz Szmuk, shall live on, and so that coming generations shall take the lessons of the Holocaust to heart, so that they will never have to experience anything like what I have been through.

Teenagers often struggle with questions about the meaning of life. One does, sometimes, even without having lived through war and persecution. I would like to paraphrase the Somali author Nuruddin Farah, who says that the meaning of life is to do good, to do good deeds, to help your neighbour — for this makes you feel good too.

Me, I believe that the meaning of life is life itself.

'Do you feel Swedish?'

The question of whether I feel Swedish is very complicated. It raises many other questions: who am I, where do I feel at home, where do I belong? Is it the place where I was born, or the place where I grew up? Is it where I have my family or my work, or is it to do with the national, ethnic, or religious group I fit into? Reaching an answer takes time.

I was born in Romania, in a Hungarian-speaking Jewish family. As a child, it was natural that other children spoke other languages, ate other food, and wore other clothes; we played together and understood each other. It was only in school that I became aware of how some considered certain groups to be better than others. We were punished for speaking languages other than Romanian. My first memory from my first day of school is receiving several lashes over my palm with a reed that left deep, red marks. Over the following years, I avoided more beatings, but was often deprived of my weekly allowance when I was caught speaking Hungarian. We were fined one leu for every word. The intention was to use the whip to make Romanians out of all these different ethnic groups. And, in part, it succeeded. When the Hungarians entered Transylvania in 1942, I was a fully-fledged Romanian nationalist. And now the Hungarians would try to turn us into Hungarian nationalists. They even used the same device — the whip.

When I came to Sweden, I did not know who I was. I came from a world where we did not count as human beings. The remarkable thing is how easy it is to see yourself through the eyes of others. If the other thinks that I am good, I feel good; if the other thinks that I am bad, I feel bad. Just like everyone else, I needed to see affirmation in the Swedes' eyes before I could answer the question of who I was. I came from Transylvania, a part of Hungary then, so I was classed as a Hungarian Jew. But the Hungarians were our hangmen, they were the ones who delivered us up to the Germans. So I did not want to profess myself a Hungarian Jew.

As a child, I wanted to see myself as Romanian. But there was only rejection in the eyes of our Romanian neighbours. Neither did I become Hungarian after the arrival of the Hungarians. I experienced that same rejection, regardless of what I might have wished for. When I arrived in Sweden, I was nothing. Would I be able to become Swedish? I hoped so. As long as I learned the language, and found work, I thought perhaps I could.

A feeling of belonging arises as a result of the interplay between the receiving community's openness and one's own will to adapt. The will to adapt was present in me from the beginning. It was wonderful to feel welcomed by Swedish society when we arrived in Malmö, but unfortunately it would not last long. With time, I discovered that I had mistaken the pity of the individuals who received us for a welcoming. It took me several years to understand. By then, I already had a job and had begun to learn the language. I was still considered a foreigner, and would remain so until I became a citizen. I found out that you did not become Swedish until you received citizenship, for which you had to wait seven years.

The years went by, I married and had three children. By now, I was rooted — I had my home in Sweden and had begun to consider myself Swedish. But Swedish society was of a different opinion; I was still just an immigrant. Me and my husband, who was also of the same origins, worked hard and contributed to the development of Swedish society.

Today, I consider myself to be Swedish, but still don't dare to say it out loud in front of people I do not know, as it is all too painful to be rejected with a look that says, 'You're not one of us. You're an immigrant, we might be able to accept that you are an immigrant Swede.'

Still, things have changed a little since the time of our arrival. Now, more and more people approach me without that doubtful look that says, 'What are you, you're not one of us?' More and more people have let go of their prejudices, and I hope that still more will, that Sweden becomes a country where we have done away with the ingrained prejudices that prevent acceptance of the other, that Sweden will embrace shipwrecked people and incorporate them into society. If immigrants and Swedes can meet halfway, we will all flourish.

'Do you see yourself in today's refugees?'

I came to Sweden in the summer of 1945, thanks to the government's generous promise to receive 10,000 sick survivors for six months' rehabilitation. Those six months turned into a whole long life filled with struggles, failures, and successes.

We were the refugees of the past, grateful for the generosity that was shown to us. To regain our human dignity, we wanted to start working as soon as we had the strength. What kind of work did not matter, we took what was offered. We thought that if we learned the language we would be able to achieve our deepest wish, to become useful citizens. We knew that we did not want to return to our former home countries, so we were not unlike the refugees of today. The only difference was that we did not want to, and today they are not able to.

When I see the shocking pictures of ramshackle, overcrowded boats on the Mediterranean, I can see myself sitting there. I too would have climbed into that boat, even with little hope of surviving. These people know that they are not welcome anywhere, just as we knew that Jews were not welcome as early as 1938. Even after 1945, it did not get any better; prejudice is like a stubborn stain, hard to wash out.

Prejudice begins as a social construction that seeks affirmation. Like a self-fulfilling prophecy, it becomes a vicious circle.

Despite this, Sweden opened up, at least for us 10,000.

When I look at today's refugees, I identify with these hapless people whose only alternative to imminent death is a dangerous journey into the unknown. Instead of being met by a helping hand, they are met by high walls and indifferent people who have lost their humanity. I see the same egotism and irresponsibility that existed in the beginning of the 1930s, but even stronger.

Then, as now, there were not many who could imagine something bad happening to themselves. The German Protestant pastor Martin Niemöller did not believe it either, as Hitler did not touch the Protestant Church in the beginning. Later, when he was imprisoned, he said: 'First they came for the communists, and I did not speak out — because I was not a communist. Then they came for the Jews, and I did not speak out — because I was not a Jew. Then they came for me — and there was no one left to speak for me.'

The worst can happen to each and every one of us, no matter how hard we try to tell ourselves otherwise. We have not yet seen the end of the refugee crisis that is taking place today, and cannot say that we, one day, will not also have to pick up the walking stick and search for a new home. If you have been through it once, you know that it can happen again.

'Have you ever been threatened by neo-Nazis?'

Some thirty years ago, I received a call from a journalist, who wanted me to discuss the Holocaust on television with one of the leading Nazi figures of the time. He was a Holocaust denier, just released from prison. I refused. I can only speak of what I have been through; I cannot convince those who do not believe me. When they argue that no one has seen a gas chamber from the inside, I can only concur. No, it is true, no one has seen a gas chamber from the inside, as no one who has walked into a gas chamber has come out alive.

It can be difficult to change the minds of inveterate Nazis, but the important thing is to reach young people before they are affected by the ideology of hate. To reach the 'tail', those who join the Nazis because it seems like a fun idea. Can young people take what happened during the Holocaust to heart? Is it possible to prevent them from joining Nazi groups who lure them in with camaraderie, music, alcohol, and the promise of adventure?

As an example of how difficult it is to get through to already dedicated Nazis, I want to tell the story of a meeting between Judith, a survivor, and an anonymous, very young Nazi who distributed leaflets with the message 'Auschwitz never happened'. Judith went up to him and asked how he could know that, seeing as he was so young when it happened. The Nazi replied that he had heard it from a renowned professor. Judith lifted the sleeve of her coat and revealed her tattooed number, A-51792. The Nazi simply laughed and said that Judith could have done that herself.

My own closest encounter with a neo-Nazi was at the beginning of the 1990s, when he was put on trial for defamation. He wrote hateful letters to various people, including me. I was called as a witness and asked to tell my story. He was sentenced to prison, but even from there he managed to send me an ugly letter. I turned it over to the police. What happened next, I do not know.

The principal of a school in Täby, Sweden, once called and asked me to come and lecture there, as some disruptive children were fighting and scrawling swastikas on the walls. After my talk — which, naturally, these boys did not attend — a few girls came up and thanked me. They thought that it was important to hear my story, and now said that they were not going to hang out with these boys any more. When the boys lost their support, the school became calmer, the swastikas disappeared.

I have received some insulting and at times threatening letters over the years. I usually hand these over to the police. They could never scare me. The goal of the anonymous letter-writers is usually just to instil fear.

'Do you hate the Germans?'

Our working party had just returned to the camp after a hard and rainy day out among the ruins. Most of us had worn our shoes out, and now rumours were circulating about a new shipment. Who would get them? Hungry and cold, with wet feet in shoes that were shoes in name only, I approached the camp chief and asked whether I could have a pair. He looked at me with an ironic grin and slapped my left cheek so hard that it left a ringing in my ear. I was close to falling over when the next slap landed on my right cheek. Instead of restoring my balance, it threw me to the ground. The pain was overshadowed by a raging hatred; I wanted to pounce on him and hit him over and over again. But I did not dare. He held the power.

Being from Hungary, I had two objects of hatred: the Germans and the Hungarians. The Germans were our tormenters, but it was the Hungarians who had handed us over to our executioners. And after the war, it would take time before I had finished hating. Strangely enough, my hatred went away quicker for the Germans than for the Hungarians. The image of the feathered hats of the Hungarian *gendarmes* would haunt me for a long time in my nightmares.

I only got over these nightmares thanks to a Hungarian immigrant who I met a few years ago. He told me that he had been born in a small village on the Hungarian *Puszta*, and had never seen a Jew until he came to Sweden. However, he knew that Jews should be hated for crucifying Jesus. He had learned this from the priests at Sunday School, before he could read.

It made me think, and eventually see the other side of the coin. I began to realise that it was not our neighbours in Sighet who had taken us to the cattle cars, it was young country cops who nourished an inculcated hatred. The rest of Sighet probably did not take a spiteful pleasure in getting rid of us. A few of our neighbours had even tried to help. My mother's hairdresser defied the ban on entering the ghetto, and visited us with groceries.

Hate is a natural reaction to being wronged, and it must be accepted for what it is. However, you do not get far with hatred, it is very counterproductive. Hatred does not affect the hated, but the one who hates feels terrible. It arouses vengeful feelings, and if these are acted upon the hated will soon become the one who hates. It leads to a never-ending spiral of hatred. It takes time before you can let go of the feeling of hatred, you have to process what happened, finish hating. Then you can move on and live without bitterness. It is not a matter of forgiving. I cannot forgive on behalf of those who were murdered, as the famous Nazi hunter Simon Wiesenthal said. But you can learn to live with what has happened. You can live side by side with the former enemy, tolerating each other. Realising that you will never know how you, yourself, would have reacted in a vulnerable situation. While I was in the camps, I hated all Germans, I was filled with vengeful feelings. Had I been given the opportunity, I would probably have taken my revenge. But after liberation, I and most of the others understood that vengeance would only make us sink to the same level as the murderers.

After the liberation of Bergen-Belsen, the British soldiers rounded up our former guards in a truck and drove around with the exhortation, 'Here you have your executioners, do as you please, take your revenge.' There were not many who did so. Most simply walked away, content with knowing that they no longer ruled over us.

Our revenge is that we, who were supposed to be exterminated, still live and have new families. Our revenge is that the Nazis of the past are gone; today, more and more of their descendants listen to our stories and work to make sure that it will never happen again.

Today, I have many friends among both Germans and Hungarians — many of them the children of perpetrators — who work towards the same goal I do.

Unfortunately, I sometimes also meet others who once again devote themselves to prejudiced ideologies of hate. They do not listen to my story, they simply repeat the rehearsed phrases that they try to spread among young people. These neo-Nazis must be isolated in order to prevent more from joining them.

Sometimes, there is a person in one's circle of acquaintances who speaks with prejudice. When that happens, I very much want to ask what they base their conviction on. With this, I hope to awaken their will to scrutinise their own and others' opinions and make their own judgement about their truthfulness. I open up a discussion that may not yield immediate results, but if a question is raised several times, it may hopefully lead to change.

'Have you met a perpetrator?'

After the war, the hatred towards the Germans stayed with me. It took time to get rid of it. What also lingered was an unconscious fear. A few years after the war, I travelled by night train through Germany, and awoke clammy with sweat from a nightmare in which the Germans were about to hang me. I woke up panic-stricken. It took me a moment to realise that it was just a dream caused by my nightdress, which had become tangled around my neck.

In the beginning, I refused both to speak German and to travel to Germany. Later, when I ran a small company and had no choice, it became very difficult. I viewed everyone my age or older as a potential perpetrator. I never allowed myself to get drawn into a private conversation; all were convicted without a hearing. It would take many years before I understood that it was prejudiced of me to see all Germans as perpetrators. I finally freed myself from suspicion and hatred. As the years went by, I started to accept invitations to various events in Germany, and found it easier and easier to socialise with German people. I even made friends. One of them was the son of a perpetrator, Martin Bormann, Hitler's right-hand man. His name was also Martin.

Like many young people, he too had been a member of *Hitlerjugend*, and by the end of the war he was fighting at the front. He was utterly miserable when Hitler surrendered. He planned to take his own life, and wandered around in the woods with a gun, without food, for several weeks. But his hunger compelled him to knock on the door of a cottage. It was home to a priest. My friend introduced himself by a different name, and asked for food. When the priest asked him questions, he told him that his father had died at the front, and that his mother was missing. The priest took pity on Martin, and he was allowed to stay there for several years. It was the first time that Martin had encountered the message of love, and it made an impression on him. He realised then the difference between the two ways of life he had experienced, and decided to spread the message himself.

Martin was not the only one who distanced himself

from the past. I met more and more young Germans who were at odds with their parents' generation, and it became their goal to put the crimes of their elders to rights.

Joakim was a young business acquaintance whose life story also moved me. He was fatherless, and convinced that his father had died at the front, like so many of his generation's fathers. His mother remarried a former military man, and soon had new children. He grew up in a loving environment, but was coloured by the Nazi spirit that still prevailed in his family. He remembered his grandmother's words, 'Whatever you do, never marry a Jewess.'

He could not quite remember when he first heard that his father had been a perpetrator. He asked his grandmother, who confirmed his affiliation to the Nazi Party, a requirement for all Germans back then. However, she did not want to admit that the father had committed any crimes.

When Joakim grew older, the accusations that his father was one of the Nazi criminals who had fled from justice after the war became more frequent. He denounced this as a lie, and hired a lawyer to prove it. The lawyer investigated, and to Joakim's great despair, he confirmed the allegations. His father had been a high-ranking officer who was responsible for the extermination of the Jews in one of the Ukrainian territories. At the end of the war, he had received help through the Catholic Church to escape to Italy, to await his entry visa to Argentina. When Joakim found all of this out, he cut all ties with his family, and decided to dedicate his life to fighting Nazism.

I met another young man, Friedrich, on the way to a conference about human rights. During the course of our conversation, it became clear that he had been a member of *Hitlerjugend* and now he was trying to straighten out his past, to get answers to why he had never thought for himself, always obediently accepting and carrying out what he was commanded to do.

He asked me about my background and was shocked when he found out that I had been in the camps. I did not want to know more about his past, where he had been and what he had done. Now that he participated in the same work as I did, the past was unimportant. Only if former enemies can unite and fight together for the same goal can we hope for a better future, a future in a dignified society, a life without hate and without vengeance.

'Are you able to forgive?'

This is a question I have thought about often, until I realised that you do not have to think in those terms. What has been done may not be undone, time cannot be turned back, those who are gone will never come again. Today, we have to look to the future.

What we can do today is work to make sure that it never happens again.

'Have you travelled back to your hometown?'

I had to put up with nightmares for a long time. When I was married and had children, I dreamed at night that I was in Sighet, and that my family was still in Stockholm. I thought that I would never dare to go back there.

But time passed and my children grew, and when they became aware of what was special about our family, they asked questions. After all, they had no maternal or paternal grandparents, no aunts on their father's side, no extended family with whom they could spend the school breaks as their classmates did. No special occasions where the entire family got together. When they entered their teens, I decided that we would travel to Sighet, so that they would feel closer to their roots and understand our situation a bit better.

During the journey, it was a very difficult task to tell my own children about our family who had been lost. I did not want them to see that I was sad, so I talked as if I was a tourist in a foreign city, turning the pages of a book written by someone else. I did not let myself feel anything. I did not yet understand that listing facts yields only intellectual knowledge, which reaches one's mind. For emotional understanding, the story must reach one's heart. My children got the answers to their questions, but I did not know what they really thought. I was left with no real experience of having revisited my childhood home. That is why I decided to travel there again, to go on a pilgrimage with my sister, visit all the places that were important to us, let the emotions wash over us, let ourselves cry. And the following summer, we did.

Our first excursion was to the central parts, where the park was lined with shops. It was like going to the theatre, watching a play I had already seen. The scenery was the same, but the actors had all changed. The music pavilion in the park was still there, but newly rebuilt. The signs outside the shops had changed; instead of the Jewish names, they now flaunted Romanian ones. I went into the shop that had previously been owned by my uncle, where an unknown owner sold the same kinds of fabrics that I used to choose from. I walked around town and saw my aunt round a street corner, but when I caught up with her it was a complete stranger.

Our old house was still there. The owners looked at us a bit suspiciously when we said that we had lived there as children. They were afraid that we wanted to reclaim it, but they let us go inside and look around. Inside, I did not see what was in front of me. Instead, I saw my parents' bedroom as it had been furnished back then. In my room I saw my most cherished possessions, the piano and the books. I could almost hear our dog Bodri barking out in the yard. Both Livi and I shed many tears. We felt like children from a storybook who had left home without permission, and were now getting a taste of the consequences — although we knew rationally, of course, that we had not been to blame.

Both of these trips brought something positive. The nightmares loosened their grip. They did not cease, but with time I stopped waking up sweaty, with a feeling that my children were still in Sweden and I was far away, that I would never see them again. It made me understand that one's fears must be confronted. Only then can you force the monsters out from under the bed.

'How often do you think about your time in the camps?'

I have lectured about my time in the different camps almost daily since the 1980s, and each time I talk about it, it feels like reliving it. Despite being very difficult, it has led to something good — it became a way for me to process my trauma.

Most survivors find it difficult to talk about what happened to them, and so it lingers as a constant ache. Because I work with it daily, talk about it, and write books about it, it is no longer there when I let go of my work. It is not present in my consciousness, though it is there under the surface, and not much is needed for it to rise up.

If I walk down the street and hear a dog barking behind me, I am back in the camp instantaneously. In the group of girls in rows of five on their way to work, guarded by SS soldiers with dogs. If someone stops, or falls out of line, we know that they will set the dogs on her. I can feel the fear, and the icy wind that blew through my thin dress, and the pain in my raw feet caused by my rough-hewn clogs. Other times, I see a chimney and feel the pain I felt when I understood what function the chimneys in Auschwitz served.

When I am with my sister, we rarely talk about the Holocaust. But what calls up the past is the same for her, and we only have to look at each other to know that we are having one thought.

'How does it feel to grow old?'

I twitch at night, and note with satisfaction that the flight I was supposed to be on has been delayed. I still do not know whether this is all a dream or whether I am really about to embark on a journey. But since the plane has been delayed, it feels good. I can look forward to yet another sunny autumn day. Am I dreaming, or is this real?

In the camps, I tried to imagine that the nights with their dreams were reality, and that the day was the dream instead. Is it so now? What am I struggling with? The answer lies in broad daylight: ageing.

When does one begin to grow old? Today, it starts later and later. Today, we speak of young seniors — that is, pensioners who still have the strength to perform. But that strength dwindles over time, and young seniors turn into old seniors. It is a very individual thing

— one's biological age does not always correspond with the age one feels. I, myself, did not begin to think about my age until my eighty-second birthday. That was when it struck me that I was old, I was turning 82. I started playing around with the numbers, and suddenly I realised that it had been ages since I turned 28.

Ageing has its pros and cons. The most difficult thing is learning to accept the slow loss of one's abilities. It starts with the deterioration of your sight and hearing, and continues with various physical and mental shortcomings. Everything slows down, you grow slower in your movements, your reactivity worsens. It is no longer advisable to drive.

At first, I became angry with myself for not having the strength to accomplish as much as before, but slowly I understood that I had to accept it and learn to slow down. In the beginning, I tried to compensate for my losses by doing things with greater attention, and more patience, but I came to the conclusion that this did not help. Your short-term memory disappears, it becomes increasingly difficult to remember people's names. It feels as if my self has lost the connection to my brain, it does not want to yield up the right answers no matter how hard I try. I notice how things that used to be of utmost importance to me have lost their significance. Over the years, it has felt like climbing up a mountain, and as you reach higher peaks, you can see everything below becoming smaller and smaller, until it is barely visible.

I no longer get worked up about trivial things, I can be forgiving of stupid statements, and accept unfair allegations to avoid conflict. My own person does not feel as important any more. Every morning, I rejoice in the new day, in the changes of the seasons, in kindness from a fellow human being. It becomes increasingly important to meet people; I, who have always been a lone wolf, now enjoy company.

When I came upon the research into gerotranscendence, I began to understand myself better. Life changes all the time, and you barely notice when you pass over the line between one stage and another. Babies grow into toddlers, children into teenagers, women go through menopause, and death is the final passage. Death is something that awaits us all, yet it is taboo to talk about it. The body prepares for it, slows down, gets new perspectives. This is what the scientists are calling gerotranscendence. The thought of death comes ever closer, and it manifests in dreams, which are more and more often about movement, about journeys, about things that one forgets to bring.

Death does not scare me. I have lived a long life, longer than I could have imagined, and everything comes to an end sometime. People leave us, new ones arrive. I have realised that there is no explanation to why we are here on Earth. What matters is how we fill our days, so that those who come after us can carry on in a better world than the one we live in now.

'After everything, do you believe in God?'

Is it possible to believe in God after the Holocaust? That is a question that many authors and philosophers have pondered and written about. If you ask those who survived, you notice that each person reacts in their own way. Many who were of deep faith before the war say, 'If this could happen, I no longer believe in God.' I remember a religious woman in the cattle car on the way to Auschwitz, who asked her neighbour if she could try some of the ham she'd brought with her. On the other hand, there were a lot of atheists who became deeply religious after the war. They became profoundly convinced that it was God who helped them to survive.

Many of the deeply religious orthodox women I was with in the camps never lost their faith. One day, they came back from working in the ruins, joyful to have found a book of prayers. They prayed every morning and every night. They fully and firmly believed that the God who helped them to escape the gas chamber would continue to help them if they followed His commandments. Despite continual searches, they managed to keep their book of prayers and followed the religious commandments even when it was difficult. They managed to calculate the date for the Day of Atonement, the day when one must neither eat nor drink. There was never a question of whether or not they would fast. On empty stomachs, without even rinsing their mouths, they got in line for the march to the work site. Once there, they toiled away all day with the heavy sacks of cement without even wetting their lips.

Faith can be helpful on life's journey, regardless of one's religion. The danger appears when it goes too far and man gets into his head that everyone must share his faith. That is when faith has turned into fundamentalism, and the original commandment of love has been turned into a commandment of hate.

In the camp, there were a few atheists who laughed at the believers, while also demanding respect for their own non-belief. They had a hard time learning that tolerance must go both ways. I cannot demand tolerance of my faith if I do not tolerate yours.

For me, nothing has changed my previous attitude. I have kept the same faith that I had before the Holocaust. I was raised Jewish and have remained a Jew. But I do not believe that my God is special. If there is a God, it is the same God that we all share, whether we use the name Jehovah, Christ, or Allah. I don't believe that God can be in heaven and watch over each and every one of us, telling us how we should act. God is found deep inside us, in the moral compass that helps us solve life's problems.

The Golden Rule, 'Do unto others as you would have them do unto you', can be found in all religions and in all languages. If all people decided to be led by it, we would live in a better world.

'What is your view of the future?'

I do not believe that my view differs from others' when thinking about how the world looks today. I see the political turn to the right, rising anti-Semitism, xenophobia, and environmental destruction. Opening the newspaper in the morning is enough to give you nightmares.

And yet, I am hopeful.

Looking at past centuries, back to the beginning of time, you see that a period of strife is often followed by a period of peace and prosperity. It has meant forward progress, but along the shape of a spiral. At the moment, we are not in a good place, but things will turn; soon we will move upwards again.

I am often asked, 'How can we avoid this happening again?' I can only think of one way, and that is through the upbringing of our children. Upbringing generally, and education particularly. Schools play a very important role in determining what tomorrow will look like. Teachers are usually innovative, and think tank meetings can broaden the way the Holocaust is taught. Good teachers become students' role models. In a crisis situation further down the road in life, this can make a big difference.

When I look at the young people of today, I feel optimistic. They have become much more self-aware, well informed, and interested in the world than we were at their age. I have an unshakeable belief that they have the will and the potential to solve today's problems.

When I meet young people, I am struck by how they have changed during the years that I have been out lecturing. They have gone from showing little interest to becoming more and more inquisitive. They ask more questions. They acquire knowledge with both their minds and their hearts; their understanding moves through both intellect and emotion.

At the end of my lectures, I am usually told by students, 'Don't worry, we will pass on what you've told us, we don't want it to happen again.'

I also believe that the school authorities have begun to understand how important it is to pursue a continuous struggle against oblivion, and that bodes well. If people of all colours, all creeds, all ethnicities, and all ages close ranks against those who do not understand how well off they are in our democracy, we will be able to hold on to what we have.

'What can we learn from the Holocaust?'

I have experienced a lot and managed to reach an advanced age. Written books, newspaper articles, and lectured for over 30 years. What I have always wanted to say, and still do, is: learn from others' and my experiences. It is a difficult art, but it is the only way to be spared the pain that we were subjected to during the Holocaust.

A German countess, daughter of the Spanish ambassador whose home was a meeting place for Hitler's opponents, said in 1948 that the world has learned nothing from either the murderers, the victims, or the onlookers. Our time is like a dance with death, and few are those who understand its strange rhythm.

The words ring true today more than ever. But we must never accept this or allow ourselves to become comfortable with it. We must not give up the fight, we must continue to spread knowledge, to help new generations grasp the rhythm, and thereby avoid the mistakes of older generations.

What is the rhythm? Charismatic leaders exploit the people's discontent with present circumstances. They offer simple answers to complex questions, and a utopian future of eternal happiness. These false prophets sound so convincing that it is easy to become ensnared. Only far later does one notice that these promises came at a price. No hopes were fulfilled, and you lost both your freedom and your home. That which you felt discontented with at the beginning becomes something you now look back on with longing. The Germans exchanged the Weimar Republic for Hitler's thousand-year dream, which led to ruin. Going back to 1914, we see how both German and French young men marched into war rapturously, only to, after four years in a ruined Europe, say with remorse, 'No more war'. And today, we are once again discontented with the state of things — where will it lead us? Where and when did it really begin?

When we look backwards, back to the dawn of history, we see how times of violent wars have been followed by a calm, bright period, only to soon darken again and end in another war. Where can we find the origin of this pattern?

I think it began when there was first reason to use the concepts 'us' and 'them'. And with that, we move back to primitive man who formed the first farming communities. Families lived separately, without contact with each other, and as they grew and felt a need for more space, they lifted their gaze to the neighbouring community. By conquering 'their' land, 'we' had space to breathe, and there was a period of calm before society grew once again. Man is selfish by nature — first there is 'me', then there is 'us', and the others are 'they', the foreign, those we do not know, those who do not concern us.

The years went by, the population of the earth increased, and while the human brain developed, our behaviour remained the same. With time, the increasing demand for living space gave birth to colonialism; it expanded ever more. To ease the conscience of the white, theories of race began to spread, taking Darwin's findings among animals as their model.

What have I learnt that I want to pass on? First and foremost, that all human beings are alike. This I learnt the hard way, through experience.

When I was a child, it was natural that there were

gentlefolk and servants. We were not rich, but there was always a maid who carried out the housework. She got up early in the morning to make a fire, so that we would not have to be cold at breakfast. I still remember the ice flowers on the window that slowly melted while the servant girl dressed me with gentle hands. I too made use of her, even though I had already become a teenager. It was the time in the camps that taught me that this had been wrong, and that we must never let it happen again. No one should have power over another, neither money nor ethnicity must be a reason to treat someone badly.

During previous centuries, some have acquired more land, and thereby more power. The powerful subdued the poor and the weak, and as a result people were sorted into categories of better and lesser. At the beginning of the nineteenth century, the misconception began to spread that humanity could be divided into different races. It turned into prejudices that still remain today. Prejudices are difficult to fight — man's inborn egotism means that we all want to feel like the best, better than others. There were many Swedes who were proud to count themselves among the Aryans when Hitler claimed that the Nordic-Germanic race was better than all the others.

Jews and Roma are two groups who have been targeted by prejudice since the beginning of time. Growing up, I had to live with prejudices against us Jews, and at the same time it was natural to me that Roma were inferior to us. It would be a long time before I came to recognise my own prejudice. By then I was already in Sweden, living in Dalarna, and had three little children.

One day, my two-year-old went missing, and no matter how hard I looked I could not find him. I became very worried, and went over to the neighbour who said, 'There was a band of gypsies that passed through, perhaps they took him.' I could not help believing her. Only when the child appeared from out of a blackcurrant bush did I understand that it was the old prejudice that was stirring up trouble when I took the neighbour's words seriously.

It is important to recognise one's own bias. One way is to, as soon as you feel a dislike for someone, ask yourself why? To scrutinise yourself and trace the origin of the feeling. Prejudices form the basis of feelings of hatred, racism, anti-Semitism, anti-Romanyism, and Islamophobia, feelings that can sometimes arise from someone in that group having caused us harm in the past. But you have to get to know a person to be able to

judge her. We are by instinct afraid of the unfamiliar —
it is a primitive feeling in man. In the beginning of time,
when people lived in small farming communities, this
was life preserving; the unfamiliar could be dangerous.
But today it is counterproductive.

Each and every one of us has a responsibility,
both to the society we live in and to ourselves. People
were no different in the 1930s or 1940s than they are
today, the same types live on. This is best observed in
the schoolyard. There are the perpetrators, the bullies
who deliver the blows, and the victims, and the ones
who simply watch without stepping in, the bystanders.
Hopefully, there are also some who come to the victims'
aid. That you should not be a perpetrator is self-evident,
but neither must you be a bystander; it makes you just
as guilty.

Today, we live in a democracy. Even though it is
not perfect, there is no other form of government that
is better. We must fight for our democracy every day if
we are to keep it, otherwise it may easily happen that
discontent with its negative aspects will produce a
charismatic leader that will put Europe in danger once
again. We must not sink down into defeatism, we must
continue to fight, despite the negative picture that the
world presents today.

'Could it happen again?'

What has happened once may happen again, not in the same way but with similar results.

Looking back on the course of history, we can conclude that just one generation is enough for the experiences of the past to pass into oblivion. We know that the Holocaust was not the first extermination of so called 'subhumans'. It was, however, the first to be given the name 'genocide' and see its instigators punished.

Under colonialism, the belief in the superiority of the white man flourished, and the murder of natives with impunity was the rule rather than the exception. A veritable extermination took place in German southwest Africa (now Namibia) at the beginning of the twentieth century, when the Germans carried out great cruelties to get rid of more than 80 per cent of the native Herero people. Many scientists argue that Hitler later looked to this as a model.

People were persecuted and murdered with impunity, and it was not until the beginning of the twentieth century that a young Polish law student by the name of Raphael Lemkin began to ponder that this should have legal consequences. But first, it must be given a name. He coined the word 'genocide' (the murder of a people) from the Greek '*génos*' (people) and the Latin '*cide*' (murder). He fought his entire life to see it accepted by the international community that genocide was a criminal act. Only after the Holocaust, in 1948, was this view adopted by the General Assembly of the United Nations. Today, 149 countries are members of the convention.

Despite this, fairly soon a genocide was instigated in Rwanda and a few years later in Serbia. It became clear that threats of punishment were not enough to avoid it happening again. Today, we know that something else is needed — a change in the way we raise our children.

New generations must continuously be reminded of former crimes. Those who raise the younger generation, parents and teachers, impart this knowledge to their children and students with the help of history books, monuments, and museums. But the way in which it is passed on is very important. If knowledge only addresses the mind, it is easily forgotten. It must also reach the heart, where it can awaken emotional learning. There are still a few eyewitnesses who can speak about their own experiences. We apprehend the world both with the mind and with the heart. Recent research also ascribes the heart with an intelligence that can be trained, just like the intelligence of the brain.

It is the good example set by parents and teachers that develops the heart, that can raise new generations to embrace empathy, unconditional love, and a world without hatred.

Soon, there will be no eyewitnesses left, and in order to try to prevent these horrors from happening again, our stories must be passed on. We already have a nominated day of remembrance, 27 January. I hope that this becomes a long-lived tradition, through which new generations can pass on the story and tell it in a way that reaches their listeners' hearts.

Acknowledgements

I want to thank all the students who have listened to my talks and raised these important questions. Questions are more important than answers. Only by asking questions can one gain some understanding of what it was all about.

We will never get an unequivocal answer to why the Holocaust happened. But through compiling all of these hows, whens, and whats, we can paint an image of the past, of the visible and hidden forces that led there.

After a lecture, getting up and asking questions is no easy thing. What I want to ask might be stupid, one often thinks, and refrains from doing so. But that very question can turn out to be the one that leads to understanding.